50 Ways to Love Yourself

Approaching the Heart with a Rational Mind

Sarah Cline, Ph.D.

Copyright © 2023 Sarah Cline, Ph.D. All rights reserved.

The contents of this book may not be reproduced, duplicated, or transmitted without direct written permission from the author.

Under no circumstances will any legal responsibility or blame be held against the publisher for any reparation, damages, or monetary loss due to the information herein, either directly or indirectly.

Legal Notice:

This book is copyright-protected. This is only for personal use. You cannot amend, distribute, sell, use, quote, or paraphrase any part of the content within this book without the consent of the author.

Disclaimer Notice:

Please note the information contained within this document is for educational and entertainment purposes only. Every attempt has been made to provide accurate, up-to-date, and reliable complete information. No warranties of any kind are expressed or implied. Readers acknowledge that the author is not engaging in the rendering of legal, financial, medical, or professional advice. The content of this book has been derived from various sources. Please consult a licensed professional before attempting any techniques outlined in this book.

By reading this document, the reader agrees that under no circumstances is the author responsible for any losses, direct or indirect, which are incurred as a result of the use of the information contained within this document, including, but not limited to, errors, omissions, or inaccuracies.

ISBN: 978-1-937209-13-1

Contents

Introduction 1
1. Understanding Personality Types: A Deep Dive 4
    Origins of Personality Types
    The Introvert and the Extrovert
    Cave Dwellers (CD) and Mountain Yellers (MY)
2. Understand Your Wants and Needs 15
    Write Down Your Short-Term and Long-Term Goals
    Revise Your Friend List
    Seek Out Emotional Fulfillment
    Set Boundaries with Your Loved Ones
    Deal with Unresolved Trauma
    Check in with Yourself after Meditating
    Journal Personal Growth Moments
    Respect Your Need for Occasional Space
3. Indulge a Little 36
    Pamper Yourself
    Update Your Wardrobe
    Go for a Walk
    Get That Dessert
    Spice up the Mundane (Sing, Dance, Crack Jokes)

Sample Wine
Make New Memories
Host Parties
Try a New Dish
Take a Vacation

4. Count Your Blessings 53
    Write a Happiness List
    Explore New Cultures
    Make New Traditions
    Walk Down Memory Lane When It Makes Sense
    Write Yourself Letters to Open Up in the Future
    Have a Game Night with Your Family and Friends
    Play with Your Kids
    Recognize Your Achievements and Celebrate Them
    Enjoy Time at Home

    Enjoy Social Events

5. Explore Your Inner Self 71
    Celebrate Your Emotional Strengths
    Understand That You're Human
    Explore Spirituality
    Find New Hobbies
    Become Your Own Best Friend

6. Boundaries 81
    Set Boundaries for the People in Your Life
    Have Consequences in Mind and Stick to Them
    Don't Overshare
    Practice Forgiveness
    Don't Forget "You" Time

7. Remain Grounded in Yourself While You Grow — 93
   Be a Mentor
   Clear the Clutter
   Volunteer
   Revisit Places of Significance
   Stick with Your Roots—Celebrate Holidays with Your Family
   Discuss Your Life with Family and Friends
   Don't Be Afraid to Ask for Help
   Seek Emotional Closeness with Family
   Check in on Your Growth Journals Often
   Hold Yourself Accountable for Maintaining Your Goals

8. Final Thoughts — 116
   Reflection on the Journey of Navigating the Love You Have for Yourself, No Matter Your Personality
   The Importance of Continuous Effort and Growth in Yourself
   Embracing the Dynamic Nature of Love and the Beauty of Learning through the Differences We All Have
   Encouragement to Evolve, Adapt, and Cherish Yourself—Always

Appendices — 120
   Self-Assessment Questionnaire: Determine If You're a CD, MY, or Straddler
   Personality Indicator Scores
   Cave Dweller Tendencies
   Cave Dweller Priorities
   Mountain Yeller Tendencies
   Mountain Yeller Priorities

About the Author

About the Author

Introduction

Welcome to *50 Ways to Love Yourself*. If you've picked up this book, it's likely because you feel some kind of inner turmoil surrounding the way you talk to yourself, see yourself, interact with the world, and show up in your relationships with others. Or perhaps you just want to deepen your personal development. Whatever drove you here, please congratulate yourself for making the first step in improving the relationship that you have *with yourself*. Yes, you read that right. Just like you're in a relationship with your significant other, your friends, and your family, you also have to work on and cultivate a relationship with yourself.

Throughout this volume and larger series, we'll focus on three universal personality categories: the reserved Cave Dweller (CD), the outgoing Mountain Yeller (MY), and the Straddler, who exhibits mixed traits. Recognizing and understanding these types is crucial, as they shape relationship dynamics in untold ways. Our aim is to provide practical insights into these fundamental personalities, ensuring you're better equipped to navigate and strengthen your relationships. What's more, you'll walk away with a better grasp of who *you* truly are—and by knowing yourself, you're better for others.

Armed with the insights from this book, you'll not only interpret your actions but also understand the deeper motivations behind them with greater ease. Prepare to understand and form a deeper appreciation for the relationship you have with yourself...

Introduction to Personality Types: CD, MY, and Straddler

Before you begin thinking deeper about the relationship you have with yourself, you first need to understand your personality type. And as mentioned before, there are three universal categories, including the CD, the outgoing MY, and the Straddler, which is a mixture of the others.

If you are a CD, you are more reserved in nature.

If you are an MY, you are more outgoing.

If you are a Straddler, you take pieces and parts from the characteristics of a CD and an MY. This means that you are probably adaptable and enjoy the best of both worlds. So, for example, you are happy to stay at home with a good book *and* to hang out with friends at a bar or restaurant.

Elucidation of CD and MY

We will focus primarily on the two opposite ends of the spectrum in this book, which are, of course, the introverted CD and the extroverted MY. So, here's a deeper explanation of what these personality types are.

If you are a CD, you exhibit the reservedness as explained above but also find yourself thinking logically, get "recharged" from time spent alone (instead of being surrounded by people), prefer to communicate with others clearly and directly, and like to focus on one thing at a time.

If you are an MY, you are the life of the party but are also driven by your emotions, get "recharged" from being around others, desire physical touch, feel the need to express every feeling and emotion you have, and communicate through storytelling, anecdotes, and metaphors instead of going directly to the point like a CD would do.

Chapter One

Understanding Personality Types: A Deep Dive

Just like any other person you are in a relationship with, you need to know, investigate, and understand your personality. And appreciating yourself means being willing to do a deep dive to see what makes you happy, makes you comfortable or uncomfortable, what makes you sad, and what makes you feel just about every other emotion.

In this chapter, we will discuss the personality types of the Cave Dweller (CD), the Mountain Yeller (MY), and the Straddler. Learning about these three basic personality types will give you a clearer picture of the unique benefits and challenges each creates. And understanding is an essential first step to bringing harmony and happiness into your everyday life.

Origins of Personality Types

Long before the modern-day classifications of CDs and MYs and even before psychiatrists and psychologists stepped onto the scene, ancient civilizations sought to explain human behavior and its various nuances.

The Ancient Greeks

The ancient Greeks developed the theory of "four humors" to explain the causes of health and illness, both mental and physical. This theory suggested that an individual's temperament was influenced by bodily fluids: blood (sanguine), yellow bile (choleric), black bile (melancholic), and phlegm (phlegmatic). The Greeks thought these humors were directly related to being sanguine (cheerful), choleric (short-tempered), melancholic (reserved), or phlegmatic (relaxed). Therefore, the balance of these humors was believed to influence an individual's temperament, health, and overall disposition. On the other hand, an imbalance of these humors led to behaviors that, today, we associate with certain mental illnesses. For example:

- Sanguine (blood) was associated with cheerful, optimistic, enthusiastic personality traits. An imbalance was thought to be due to a person having too much blood in their body, which would cause a person to be overly confident and have impulsive behavior. Possible narcissistic and/or bipolar disorder.

- Choleric (yellow bile) was associated with being ambitious, passionate, and easily angered. An imbalance causes anger, irritability, or extremely aggressive behavior and rage. Possible borderline personality disorder.

- Melancholic (black bile) was associated with being thoughtful, reflective, and often sad or depressed. This imbalance was associated with melancholy and depression.

- Phlegmatic (phlegm) was associated with being calm, reliable, and often unemotional or apathetic. An imbalance was associated with lethargy, sluggishness, or a lack of motivation, which, much like melancholic, was a symptom of depression.

Treating these emotional ailments is where things got even more interesting. If the Greeks thought you had an imbalance of any of these four humors, you would likely have received one of the following treatments:

Dietary Changes: Prescribed depending on the humor in excess. For instance, someone deemed overly choleric might be advised to avoid hot or spicy foods that would "agitate" the yellow bile.

Bloodletting: If you were someone believed to have an excess of sanguine humor, it was common practice to be prescribed bloodletting. This process involved removing blood from the body by way of leeches or actual cutting.

Purging: In order to remove excess bile or phlegm, laxatives were used, as were emetics, which induced vomiting.

Baths/Sweating: To promote toxin removal, balms and ointments were applied to the skin to help with the imbalance of any of these four humors.

The Greeks' attempts to "treat" imbalances in personality or health were based on the observations and the knowledge they had at the time. The four humors theory was eventually replaced with more accurate medical models, but its influence can still be seen in some of our languages today.

The Introvert and the Extrovert

Carl Gustav Jung (1875-1961) was a Swiss psychiatrist, psychoanalyst, and the father of analytical psychology. He developed several concepts that had a profound influence on both psychology and popular culture. One of his most notable contributions was the concept of "introversion" and "extraversion" (often used in the more modern manner: introvert and extrovert). Jung's theory asserts that introversion and extraversion are attitudes that represent the direction in which a person's psychic energy flows.

Extraversion (Extrovert)

According to Jung, the extrovert's energy flows outward. This personality type is more oriented toward the external world and derives energy from interacting with its surroundings, including people, events, and situations. If you are an extrovert, you tend to be more outgoing, social, and interested in external events. You are typically action-oriented and are generally more comfortable in social situations than an introvert. Many extroverts are highly influenced by external factors and are occasionally prone to negative introspection.

Introversion (Introvert)

As the name suggests, the introvert's energy flows inward. This personality type is more oriented toward their inner world, relying on introspection and internal reflection. If you are introverted, you are generally more reserved and often feel more comfortable with individual activities or smaller group settings. You derive energy and pleasure from thinking, daydreaming, or exploring ideas. Although an introvert's daily practices tend to lead to social isolation, many have a small number of deep connections with people of their choosing.

Jung believed that everyone has an introverted and extroverted side, with one being more dominant than the other. It's a spectrum, and while some people might be near the extremes of that spectrum, most individuals lie somewhere in between.

Cave Dwellers (CD) and Mountain Yellers (MY)

While not strictly rooted in these historical contexts, the CD and MY classifications are evolved constructs reflecting the same human desire to understand ourselves and others in our world more deeply.

While our contemporary understanding of the CD and MY classifications doesn't stem directly from ancient Greek or Jungian theories, much like their historical counterparts, they are observed patterns in modern relationships. By identifying recurring patterns, you can forge tools to help you navigate and harmonize interpersonal interactions. To determine whether you fall into the CD or MY category, you must first learn about their traits.

Deeper Dive into the Cave Dwellers

Reserved Nature

If you are a CD, you will predominantly showcase a calm and reserved demeanor. You are introspective and tend to hold emotions close to your chest because you value your inner world and the sanctuary it provides. Your reserved nature doesn't mean that you are indifferent or don't care about things; it just means that you process your emotions internally and over time.

For instance, after an argument, a CD might choose to withdraw to process their feelings rather than immediately confront an issue. A CD does this because they typically feel uncomfortable with strife and need time to work through emotions and how to communicate their feelings.

Socially, a CD is often found in quieter corners, engaging in deep conversation with one or two individuals rather than in the center of a party. In group discussions, a CD will offer insights only if specifically asked or if they feel strongly about a topic.

Logical Thinking and Literal Communication

A CD leans more toward analytical and logical thinking. They make decisions only after careful contemplation and weighing the pros and cons. They work hard to keep their emotions from clouding their judgment. This logical thinking manifests in their communication, as they will get right to the point without inserting emotions or using stories to embellish their point.

For example, if you discuss a film with a CD, they will likely dissect plot points with impeccable logic and even point out strengths and weaknesses. But they often miss the emotional undertones of the movie. If you ask a CD if they liked the cake you brought for dessert, they might reply, "Yes," without diving into flowery descriptions.

It's important to note that if you are a CD, you may also get frustrated with an embellished story that doesn't immediately get to the point. It doesn't mean you don't want to hear the story or don't care what the person has to say; your brain is just geared toward immediate outcomes.

Need for Space

A CD has an inherent need for both emotional and physical personal space. For them, requiring space is not about distancing themselves from loved ones. It's about needing solitude to recharge and reflect.

A CD enjoys reading books in a cozy nook or going for solitary walks. They may listen to music while cooking dinner instead of talking. This alone time is essential for a CD, especially after a day filled with social interactions.

Singular Focus

A CD has unparalleled concentration when engrossed in a task and prefers completing that task to their satisfaction before tackling another.

If someone attempts to talk to a CD while they're writing an email, for example, they may be so absorbed in what they're writing that others will be tuned out. It's not that what someone is saying is unimportant to them; it's just challenging for them to spread their focus on more than one thing at a time because they give each item their full attention.

Social Preferences

Traditionally, if you were labeled an introvert, many would also consider you antisocial. But that couldn't be further from the truth. An introvert, or a CD, just leans toward more intimate social interactions. Large gatherings can leave a CD feeling overwhelmed and quickly drain their mental and emotional battery.

Emotional Processing

While a CD might not outwardly express their emotions, they experience them deeply. However, their internal reflections may lead to a delay in their outward emotional expression. While a CD may seem distant after an emotional confrontation, many need to process the interaction before they react. A CD needs time to contemplate a disagreement, analyze the conversation, and figure out where things went wrong before they can move on to a resolution.

Fears Regarding Loss of Security

Finally, if you are a CD, you crave stability in your life, especially regarding your finances. You will likely be frugal in your spending and make decisions with the lowest level of risk. At times, a CD may pick a job over family, not because they love to work more, but because they need security above all else. The hierarchy of basic needs for a CD is as follows:

- Career/Financial Security
- Hobbies/Children
- Relationships/Family
- Sex/Lovers

The position of each need doesn't mean they don't love and value their partner/family. It means that it's essential for a CD to feel that they're providing security for themselves and their family before they can give their full attention to the next set of needs. So, if you're a CD, communicate to those around you that your needs come first for you. It's not being selfish. That's just how your brain works and prioritizes things.

Deeper Dive into the Mountain Yeller

If you are an extrovert, chances are you've been called that more than once in your lifetime. An extrovert is typically known for being outgoing and the life of any party. But there's so much more to them than meets the eye.

Outgoing Nature/Group Socialization

An MY is inherently outgoing. Their energy thrives on interactions and being around people as often as possible. Instead of needing time alone to recharge, an MY wants to be out and involved.

At a social event, an MY will be the first to initiate games and dancing and will often bounce from person to person, catching up rather than focusing on one task at a time. Deep conversations are still on the table but not at a social event. MYs are usually the ones who rally their friends for a group outing over a weekend rather than sitting at home reading a book or watching TV. Even in the workplace, MYs love group projects and find collaborative brainstorming and teamwork exciting.

Emotion-Driven

MYs are heart-ruled because they lead with their intuition and emotions. Being ruled by their heart doesn't mean their decisions are devoid of logic, but their feelings heavily influence their reactions. MYs can be emotional during arguments but are also the first to send a heartfelt message to a friend upon hearing they are having a rough time.

An MY's emotions will show throughout their storytelling. Chances are both will be full of details and embellishments.

Connection and Touch

MYs crave genuine connections and physical touch. Whether a hug, a pat on the back, or simply holding hands. It reinforces their feeling of being connected. In a relationship, the MY will crave physical affection and see it as a top priority over other needs—something we'll discuss in depth a bit later.

Dynamic Focus

An MY is a natural multitasker. Instead of focusing on one task at a time, their attention shifts between assignments. They enjoy the energy they get from juggling multiple things and often get bored working on one project for an extended period. It can be common for an MY to drift off during a long presentation. They're busy thinking about weekend plans.

The MY doesn't mind dealing with paperwork, but they'll work through it while watching television or listening to music. As for conversations, the MY loves to chat but may also be scrolling on their phone as they talk to someone. It's not that the MY thinks what someone has to say is unimportant. Their mind simply runs at higher speeds, and they're more comfortable when processing more than one thing at a time.

Inferential Communication

The MY often communicates using stories, anecdotes, and metaphors rather than getting straight to the point. They rely on indirect implications and expect others to infer meanings, which can confuse some who may not be familiar with their communication style.

Immediate Emotional Expression

Unlike their CD counterparts, MYs are quick to express their emotions. They're an open book and rarely hesitate to share their feelings of joy and disappointment.

One of the greatest fears the MY faces is the fear of rejection. The hierarchy of basic needs for the MY is as follows:

- Relationships/Sex
- Family/Children
- Friends/Hobbies
- Career/Financial Security

Again, the position of each need does not mean that you don't value friends and finances. Moreover, it's important to know whether you're an MY or not because if you are, you'll need to make sure that you are getting all of these needs met in the order that you need or want them to be. It can also be helpful to tell your friends that your partner and family will always come first over everything else, so they know that going in.

Chapter Two

Understand Your Wants and Needs

As we've just covered, you need to know whether you're a CD, MY, or Straddler because that determines the hierarchy of needs and wants that you have. And once you've determined what those needs are, it will be much easier for you to live the life that is most suitable and beneficial for you.

Below are suggestions for ways in which you can make the determination of what matters most to you in life.

Write Down Your Short-Term and Long-Term Goals

Short-term goals can be anything from making your bed each day for an entire week and getting the dishes that have been sitting in your sink clean to getting a new certification for work. Basically, a short-term goal can be something small that you would like to get off your "checklist," and that can be done in a relatively short amount of time. And due to the nature of these goals, you will need to set them frequently (some find that sitting down one day a week and reflecting on the six days ahead to be beneficial; others do this daily or monthly). And some short-term goals require diligence, so they may feel more like long-term goals, but you can get the ball rolling by establishing a good habit today.

You should also try your absolute best to stick to these smaller goals once you make them (this builds integrity and your confidence in yourself).

Long-term goals, on the other hand, are the "big picture" things you want to achieve. That may include going to college, getting married to your partner, buying a house, or having children. These goals need a lot of effort, planning, and preparation. They cannot be done in one afternoon, one week, or even one year. They will have a lasting impact on your life. Moreover, you may want to include *when* you want to achieve these goals because that might also be important.

Here are more examples of *short-term* goals that you may have or will have in the future:

- Changing your job
- Teaching a course
- Volunteering your time
- Organizing your office or workstation
- Drinking more water
- Earning a professional certificate or attending a workshop
- Creating a new morning routine

- Trying a new recipe
- Attending a networking event
- Reading more
- Starting to budget
- Updating your portfolio
- Keeping a daily journal
- Improving your communication skills
- Decluttering your house or apartment
- Improving your self-care
- Making your own coffee every morning instead of stopping by a café
- Picking a new hobby
- Flossing more often
- Making a bucket list
- Creating daily affirmations
- Committing to saying "yes" to something that is out of your comfort zone
- Eliminating the amount of screen time you have
- Eating healthier
- Taking an exercise class

- Waking up earlier in the morning to meditate or do any other self-care routine

- Seeking mental health support

- Learning to make your favorite cocktail (or mocktail)

- Starting a garden

- Updating your resume

- Investing in stocks

- Starting a podcast

- Backing up important documents

- Cleaning out your car

And here are some more examples of *long-term goals* that you may have or will have in the future:

- Obtaining a degree or going back to school for additional degrees

- Building a professional network

- Becoming an expert in your field

- Writing a novel

- Getting a pet

- Purchasing a new car

- Becoming a successful entrepreneur

- Learning a new language
- Living abroad in a different place
- Becoming a better friend or parent
- Traveling the world
- Saving for retirement
- Paying off credit cards and loans
- Saving money for a vacation, a child's tuition, or anything else
- Increasing your physical strength and agility

Say No to Things that Don't Align with Your Goals

Whether your goals are short or long-term, once you determine what they are, you will have to make decisions that either support or prevent you from achieving them. Hopefully, you will have the foresight to see the bigger picture and determine which things will help you reach your goals.

But this isn't always easy—especially when the person asking you to do something taking you away from your goal is someone who you care about or respect. However, keep in mind that it is okay to prioritize yourself and your goals above all else (other than your other responsibilities—like paying bills, caring for children, taking care of your body, and things like that).

It's also important to note that when you say no to things that will prevent you from achieving a goal, you are also focusing your energy and your effort on that very goal. And speaking of energy, even if you technically have the time to do something, it may not be worth the mental energy that it drains from you and your work toward your goal (and by saying no, you may be opening the door to things that are actually worth saying yes to). Basically, you need to learn to trust your gut instinct. If *you* are aligned with your goal, you'll know right away when things are drifting away from it.

Achieving Short-Term Goals

Let's say your short-term goal is the dishes example given earlier. Well, say you still have not done them, and your friend calls you up and asks you to go to a movie. If you know that going to that movie will interfere with you getting those dishes done, you should probably thank them for the invite but skip it this time. That's why we said it's so important to stick to these goals because they can be easy to abandon or put off. And these less serious tasks can also contribute to your long-term goals…what if one of your goals was to have a nice, clean house someday? Getting into a habit of doing your dishes regularly will only bring you one step closer to achieving that!

Achieving Long-Term Goals

Aside from sticking to your short-term goals that either support or are completely separate from your long-term goals, you may also need to make decisions that will help you achieve the bigger ones as well.

For instance, suppose one of your long-term goals is to have a baby by the time you're thirty-five, and you're thirty-three and presented with a promotion that comes with a salary increase, and that money will help you and your partner buy the house of your dreams where you can raise a family? You should probably take the promotion if it's what is best for you in other respects of your life.

In the reverse, your long-term goal is to spend more time with a family that you already have. So, that promotion, which would likely come with more work, might be something it would be better for you to turn down.

That's why determining when you want to achieve something in consideration of all of your external circumstances needs to be so hyper-specific and catered to you and your life.

Revise Your Friend List

This can be one of the hardest things to do because many people grow up with the mentality that friends are everything. And while they are important, it's equally as imperative that you're careful to have the *right* friends in your life.

A friend should be someone who lifts you up, makes you excited to be around, and who you can trust. If you sigh every time you get a call, text, or message from a friend, it might be time for you to cut them loose. Energy suckers are a real thing.

And it doesn't even have to be a permanent thing. People have their own battles to fight and lessons to learn. Suppose your friend is in a really toxic, negative relationship, and that's what she's calling to vent to you about, and it's becoming detrimental to your mental health—it's okay to distance yourself from that person until (or if) she eventually leaves that situation.

However, sometimes, a permanent ban on the relationship is warranted.

The baseline is that if a friend isn't in your corner and supportive of you achieving your goals, it's time to evaluate whether you need that person in your life or not.

Just remember that you can't control people, so if they're engaged in a relationship or behavior you'd rather not have in the orbit of your life, it's completely fine to let them know that either a break or complete separation is necessary.

Regardless, here are a few signs to look out for that might mean it's time to move on from a friendship:

- **You are not a priority to them.** This one is a little tricky because life does get in the way of friendships sometimes—especially if your friend has children, a very stressful job, etc. However, if you continually feel like they don't really care about you or what's going on in your life, it's probably best for you to move on.

- **You don't want the same kind of connection.** Friendships work best when both parties are in it for the same thing. So, if you want a deep connection with someone, but they aren't open or willing to give that to you, it's likely better for you to try to find another friend who will.

- **Your friend tears you down.** The whole point of having friends and being a friend is to encourage and support each other. So, if you have a friend who is constantly criticizing you (for trivial things—good friends will tell you when they think you're making genuine, life-changing mistakes) and making you feel bad about yourself, that's a good sign that it's time to move on.

- **Your friend lies or hides information.** Trust is a huge part of any deep connection between one or more people. Having said that, if you notice that your friend is deceiving you or omitting facts, your relationship will likely flounder.

- **You feel the need to downplay your achievements.** If you ever feel like you need to make your accomplishments seem less impressive than they actually are in order not to hurt a friend's ego, that's a good indicator that your friend is jealous. Good friends celebrate each other's wins and want one another to succeed.

- **Your friend ignores the boundaries you put in place.** If there is a boundary you set with someone, and they repeatedly break it, that's a sign that they do not respect you and your autonomy.

- **It's all about them.** A healthy friendship is about give and take, so if you have a friend who only seems to vent their drama onto you and does not offer to help you with your troubles, consider dumping them.

- **Their values no longer align with yours.** This is not to say that you can't disagree with your friend about something, but if you have two very differing opinions and can't reach a middle ground, that may also be a sign that it's time to move on from each other.

- **They gaslight you.** If you have a friend who questions the clear identity you have for yourself, and they minimize every experience you have, it's probably best to part ways.

After you notice one of the signs above or anything else that alerts you that you're in an unhealthy friendship, here are some tips on how to end it (and the right way to go will depend on the unique situation):

- **Track and measure your screen time.**
    - Apple and Android have built-in functions—called Screen Time and Digital Wellbeing, respectively—that allow you to see just how much time you spend on particular apps on your phone. It can be very sobering to see just how much time you waste scrolling through Instagram, watching YouTube videos, etc. If you decide to go this route, make sure that you also change your auto-lock settings to be just thirty seconds…otherwise, it could make your data inaccurate.

- **Set a screen limit or use a timer.**
    - Some of the functions that were mentioned in the last bullet point can also be utilized to limit the amount of time you allow yourself to be on social media apps. However, please note that Apple's Screen Time will make you aware that you've exceeded your time, but you can extend it for fifteen more minutes or choose to ignore it altogether and keep scrolling. Whereas Android's Wellbeing app is less lenient, and when you pass the limit, the only way you can get more time is to disable the timer entirely.

- **Turn off your notifications.**
    - Either just turn off the sound and vibration of your phone or turn on the Do Not Disturb or Focus Assist functions to avoid notifications even popping up on

your screen.

- **Go grayscale.**
  - One of the reasons so many of you are addicted to your screens is because the bright colors on them trigger happiness in your brain. So, by muting them, you make the phone less enticing for you and easier to stay away from.

- **Delete or hide time-sinking apps.**
  - If you've tried the things above, but you still find that you want to constantly look at your phone, it might be easiest for you to simply delete the apps that you feel you are most addicted to. It will probably be hard to do at first, but you will only benefit from being more focused and present in the future.

- **Pursue offline activities.**
  - Another great way to stay off your phone is by adopting habits that keep you distracted from it—like hiking, getting a massage, or drawing.

- **Create screen-free spaces in your home.**
  - Say, for example, that you find it hard to fall asleep at night because you're always looking at your phone. In that case, it might be helpful to designate your bedroom as a phone- and device-free space, and you don't ever take your phone in there. This is another step that will be hard to do at first and probably stick to, but your body and mind will thank you for it later after a few good nights of sleep.

- **Avoid eating in front of your phone.**

  - When you eat and watch a movie, show, or video, it triggers a feeling of productivity in your brains that you're getting two things done at once. That's why so many of you love doing it! Stopping this habit will benefit you in two ways:

    - One, you probably find it hard to stop watching something before it's over...even when your meal is done. So, if you skip eating and watching altogether, you can inherently reduce your screen time.

    - Two, when you watch something on your phone while eating, you pay less attention to the amount of food you're consuming. So, eating away from a screen can reduce how much you actually put in your body.

Seek Out Emotional Fulfillment

This will also require you to know yourself and what makes you happy. For instance, some people find happiness in cuddling with puppies at their local shelters, and others feel like they're crawling out of their skin if they don't get their daily run in.

Whatever you need to do in order to be happy, at peace, and all the other positive emotions, you should prioritize those activities and especially incorporate them during particularly stressful times in your life. The instinct is often to push these aside in favor of work, taking care of a sick family member, or school assignments. But that simply is not the case.

Your emotional health is just as important as your physical, so it is *not* selfish for you to take the time you need to get some bursts of serotonin, dopamine, oxytocin, and endorphins (aka the happy hormones) in your brain!

Set Boundaries with Your Loved Ones

Just as you should prioritize your emotional fulfillment, you should also set very clear boundaries with your partner, family members, and friends. And those boundaries, whatever they are, are for you—and only you—to set.

It's also kind of like revising your friend list. You get to decide who, when, and how someone gets to be in your life.

Especially when it comes to family, it's good to remember that sharing blood with someone does not mean that they get to be in your life. If anyone in your family—your mom, dad, siblings, aunt, cousins—does something that you deem reprehensible, you can decide what boundaries you need to set when it comes to that person.

For example, say your aunt said something you found to be offensive to you or someone else. Depending on the circumstances, whether or not you feel comfortable enough to talk to them about refraining from using such language, and if they seem receptive to change—you can decide that it's best for you not to go out in public with them or stop associating with them altogether.

The same goes for just about anyone in your life. If they do not make you feel good, safe, and supported, you need less of them or don't need them at all.

But it's important to understand that there are also different types of boundaries.

If you have *open* **boundaries**, you are probably:

- Getting too involved in other people's business.
- A people pleaser who finds it hard to say "no" to others.
- Oversharing your personal information with others.
- Someone who fears rejection.

If you have *rigid* **boundaries**, you are probably:

- Do you share personal information appropriately (not too much and not too little)?
- Do you understand your personal needs and wants and feel comfortable communicating them to others?
- Do you value your own opinions?
- Do you accept when others tell you "no?"

Congratulations—if you answered yes to these questions, you likely have a healthy set of boundaries. However, please be aware that boundaries change given the situation and culture of the people around you. For example, in some cultures, it's never seen as appropriate to share your personal business. So, being aware of your surroundings is also required.

Deal with Unresolved Trauma

With all of the easily accessible outlets for therapy today, it's never been easier to get help from a professional therapist. What's even better, the apps and services available today make it easy to try a multitude of people before finding the right therapist that you feel is right for you.

Once you find the perfect person, they can help you interpret, analyze, and heal from trauma that you may have held onto from your childhood. Remember, if the trauma involves a person, that resentment is like drinking poison yourself and still hoping the other person will suffer the consequences of that. It's most likely only hurting you. That doesn't mean that the feelings aren't valid, but forgiveness is a gift you give to yourself in order to live a more positive and hopeful life.

And maybe you don't think you need a traditional "talk therapy." There are so many other therapies that can help people heal—like music, art, meditation, hypnosis, animal-assisted, and so, so much more. If you have an interest or hobby, there's a chance there is a type of therapy that can build on that.

The first step is just admitting that there's something you could work on moving on from the past and finding the right path of healing for you.

Check in with Yourself after Meditating

Meditation is a type of mindfulness that involves deep breathing, closing of the eyes, and being guided through a session by someone else, or just picturing things in the mind. You don't have to do it for long to reap the benefits of it.

But when you're done with your practice, you will benefit from checking in with how you feel—both mentally, emotionally, and physically.

Through this process, you may discover more areas that you need to work on during your meditation journey.

Suppose you have a headache; you may want to do another session that focuses on making that pain go away. Or you feel sad, so you want another few minutes to focus on happiness.

The mind is an incredibly powerful thing, and what you tell it to think, focus on, and do…your body will follow suit. It really is incredible.

Remember that disease is really dis-ease, and it reflects any turmoil you may have in your mind, body, and spirit. Meditation can help you heal from the inside out.

Journal Personal Growth Moments

As you're making progress in your personal development journal, you should journal and make a note of each new success.

Even if it's something little like keeping your word that you'd take the trash out that day. The fact that you committed to putting that as a goal and actually executed it deserves recognition as the growth that it is. In the future, you can use that "small" success to inspire you to continue similar patterns.

And of course, big moments should also be recorded. Suppose you made it a goal to save the money for a new laptop, and that required you to go without some of the "fun money" you were used to spending. As soon as you save up and actually purchase that laptop, you should journal about both achievements. You earned the right to brag about yourself a little bit, and it's in a format that won't rub anyone the wrong way because no one will see it (unless you want them to).

Respect Your Need for Occasional Space

This one was also touched on in the point about editing your list of friends, but it applies to everyone in your life. If you need space and time to yourself or away from a particular person, please take it.

It may seem selfish at first, but taking time for yourself or distancing from a friend, family, or anyone else should be respected without second-guessing. This applies equally to MY and CD.

Almost everyone needs some peace and quiet from time to time. Here are some reasons why you may need space from someone:

- **To maintain your identity.** Sometimes, you lose yourself in a relationship. So, when you feel like you're losing yourself, some space can help you rediscover who you are.

- **For personal development.** If you are in a relationship that you feel is keeping you from advancing as a person, taking space for yourself will show you and the other person how committed you are to being the best version of yourself that you can be.

- **To improve the health of the relationship.** They say that distance makes the heart grow fonder...it can also improve the quality of a relationship. Time alone refocuses and reconnects you to yourself. That typically leaves you more open, honest, and tolerant of those around you.

- **For emotional and mental health.** Distancing yourself from someone can help you to evaluate if you are being the best friend or partner that you can be, and it also gives you time to evaluate the other person as well.

- **Avoiding codependency.** Codependency occurs when people become too reliant upon each other for emotional validation. Time away and space can help break these cycles.

- **To build anticipation and desire.** Again, distance makes the heart grow fonder.

However, if you have trouble discerning the need for space on your own, here are thirteen signs for you to look out for:

1. **You are arguing over little things.** One of the first indications that you've had enough of someone is when you find that you are constantly battling with them over silly things that really have no impact on either of your lives.

2. **You're constantly seeking approval from someone before you do something.** No matter what kind of relationship you are in with someone, you and only you should be in charge of making your own decisions. And the reason for you always seeking external approval may have something to do with you being insecure with yourself, the other person being controlling, or a little bit of both. Time away and doing a few things without seeking approval should help—especially if your insecurity is at the root of the issue.

3. **You're annoyed by their habits.** This is another great sign

that you need some space away and to yourself.

4. **You'd rather be alone than be with them.** Of course, it is normal for anyone to want time alone sometimes, but when it's the overall majority of how you feel around your partner, family member, or friend, you may want to reevaluate the relationship and decide if you could use some space away from them.

5. **The relationship drains you.** We've mentioned energy suckers in this book before—they are the kind of people who literally, through their behavior and interactions with you, suck the energy out of you. Depending on who the energy sucker in your life is, you may want to consider getting some time away from them to recharge...either temporarily or permanently.

6. **You do not want them to join in on your hobbies.** People involved in healthy relationships typically get excited about the prospect of sharing their hobbies with friends and loved ones. So, if you find that you do not want certain people to join in on your hobby, that may be a subconscious way of you telling yourself that you need space from them. And on the reverse, if the same is being done to you, try to talk about it, but ultimately respect the boundary they've set.

7. **You suddenly change your schedule.** Like the previous point, this can also be a way for you to tell yourself and someone else that you need space. Also, if you notice someone is changing their schedule on you, try to respect that.

8. **You don't feel the need to tell someone where you are going.** This can be a clear warning sign that you don't value

the person's opinion on your daily activities.

9. **You reply to someone with short answers.** This can signal to you that you need a break from someone (or they need a break from you if you're the recipient of the short replies).

10. **You feel no need for physical affection**. If that was something that was once prevalent in your relationship, and you find that you no longer want to engage in that kind of behavior, it could be a sign that you need space from that person.

11. **You no longer feel connected to that person.** Having a relationship with anyone requires connections. So, if you no longer feel that it may be time for a break from that partner or friend.

12. **You no longer feel like you are your own person.** No matter how much time you spend with someone, you should never feel like you are turning into one—instead, you should always have your own personality, beliefs, mindset, and wishes. And if you ever feel like you're losing that, please consider taking some space to rediscover and own up to who you are.

13. **You don't like spending time with them.** The whole point of having relationships with people is because you enjoy their company. So, if you don't want to be around someone in private or in public, that's a pretty good indicator that the relationship needs to end or that you need some space away from that person.

14. **You start thinking about what your life would be like without them.** The second you start wondering what your

daily life would look like if someone wasn't in it, you should pause and analyze where those thoughts are coming from. If it's because you've had too much of them, consider getting some space.

Chapter Three

Indulge a Little

Just like buying your significant other a nice experience or gift, sometimes treating yourself is the best way to show your appreciation for your body, your health, the world, and the blessing you've been given by being alive.

In this chapter, we'll talk about a few ways in which you can spoil yourself or just change the pace of your life.

Pamper Yourself

This can involve going to a professional, like booking a massage, a pedicure and manicure appointment, a facial, a haircut, a blowout, or getting your makeup done.

But if you are on a budget or just feel like you'd rather have a DIY situation, you can pop over to your local store and find masks for your hair or your face, nail polish, manicure and pedicure tools, bath bombs or bubble bath solution, and anything else you might need for a home spa.

Especially if you're feeling like you could use a little self-love, taking the time to pamper yourself may be just the trick you need to feel more confident and ready to face the world.

Further, if you're feeling lonely or know of a friend who could also benefit from a spa day, invite someone (or multiple people) over to join you. The more the merrier sometimes, right?

Update Your Wardrobe

Another great way to make you feel more excited to get ready for work or school every day is to go to the mall or any clothing store and get some new clothes. Better yet—try a style or fashion trend you've always wanted to try but were too nervous in the past to actually do it.

And you don't need to spend a fortune. Clearance racks and thrifting are perfectly good options for this. Plus, if you pick versatile pieces that will match other clothes that you already have, that's even better.

This also goes for jewelry and accessories. Sometimes, a good necklace or pair of earrings can spruce up an outfit you are feeling tired of.

Another great way to update the clothes in your closet is by actually going the extra mile and having old and new pieces alike altered to fit your body. It might seem silly, but it really is a game changer—the clothes on the rack are designed to fit one standard size...not *your* unique measurements. And when an item of clothing fits you properly, it will minimize the damage done by the wear and tear of a poor fit (like pressure on seams and fabric). So, you're increasing the amount of time you'll be able to wear it. Still not convinced? Tailored clothes will likely also make you feel more comfortable *and* more confident.

You could also review the clothes you already own. For instance, are you undecided if you should give your clothes away? Here are eight items that you should consider getting rid of in your closet:

1. **Anything that is uncomfortable**. If it is itchy or gives you a rash, it's time for that piece (or those pieces) to go.

2. **Anything that looks worn.** This is especially true if you are a professional who needs to look nice on the job—as much as it stinks to admit this—your appearance is important. And clothes that look worn will be a mark against you.

3. **Anything you bought for yourself but simply don't wear**. If you haven't worn something in a year, you probably won't wear it. That isn't true for everything, but it's a good baseline to have.

4. **Gifts from others that you can't exchange but don't like**. You may feel obligated to hang on to pieces that were gifted to you, but if you don't like something, think of the person out there who would feel confident wearing it.

5. **An overflow of sentimental pieces**. It's okay to have some, but it's usually best to have only one or two boxes.

6. **Anything that you can't commit to having tailored**. If you've needed to sew a button on, change the hemline, or fully get an item of clothing tailored to fit your body for over three months, try your hardest to get it done that week or get rid of it.

7. **Anything that no longer matches your lifestyle**. Let's face it: you may not be the person you were when you were younger. Now, you may have kids, a remote job, so all of the

suits and party dresses in your closet may be put to better use by someone else.

8. **Anything you don't feel good in.** Clothes are supposed to elevate your look and your confidence. And especially if that latter criterion is not being met, it might be time to pitch it.

Go for a Walk

One of the simplest ways for you to take care of yourself is by getting exercise regularly, and a walk around your neighborhood is an easy way to get those daily steps in. And while you walk, you can listen to music or a podcast and get lost in the beautiful nature that is all around you.

However, if you feel like pushing yourself to be more social, skip the headphones and be open to talking with neighbors.

Moreover, if you're an animal person, have the means to afford a pet, live in a suitable environment, and want the extra motivation to get out and walk, getting a dog can really help you with that. Night or day, and no matter the weather condition (barring any dangerous situations for you and your pooch—like extreme heat or storms), they must get outside and walk, and you've got to go with them. So, it's a win-win!

Going for a walk is a prime opportunity for you to consciously feel grateful for the little things...like the sun shining down on you, the beautiful green leaves on the trees, the clean air you're breathing into your lungs, the sound of laughter from the children who are playing outside, the adorable puppy you passed.

Get That Dessert

This one is pretty self-explanatory, but another great way to show love for yourself is by allowing yourself to enjoy the delicious foods that you crave and enjoy most. Be it ice cream, cookies, pie, cake, or whatever, just go out and get yourself some! Life is too short to always inhibit yourself from the things you love most.

Spice up the Mundane (Sing, Dance, Crack Jokes)

If you're feeling like you're in a vicious cycle of "blah," any easy way to change that is by having fun. So, don't be afraid to go to the club and dance your heart out, go to karaoke with friends, or maybe even try something as courageous as stand-up comedy.

Whatever you choose to do, just enjoy it, and even if you feel like you stink at dancing, singing, and/or telling jokes, who cares? If you feel happy, that's all that matters.

You know the saying dance like nobody is watching? Embrace that to the fullest. Because at the end of the day, does it really matter what anyone thinks of you? No. And honestly, most people think others are paying closer attention to them than they really are.

If stand-up seems too daunting for you, start by slipping some jokes in when you're around your friends. Starting small is an accomplishment in and of itself.

Consider these activities as live-action studies in human joy and resilience. Just as a researcher tests hypotheses, you too are exploring the boundaries of your comfort zone. Each step, note, or joke is a data point in your personal growth chart. Life, after all, is the most vibrant of laboratories…and the goal is to find what bring you bliss.

Sample Wine

Another place you can broaden your horizons is by learning about the finer things in life—such as wine. You never know what you like until you try it and give yourself a grace period. For some, wine is an acquired taste, and it takes a while for them to develop a taste for it. If that's you, that's totally fine. Try it a few more times, and if you still don't like it…maybe you just don't like wine.

However, if you have developed the taste or already know that you like it, sampling is an inexpensive way to try different wines—from reds, whites, spicy, fruity, sweet, dry—and also potentially meet people who share the same interests as you.

You'll also probably learn new "fancy" things like the level of tannins, body, and acidity that are in particular types of wine.

But please make sure you're always drinking responsibly and order a rideshare of some kind when going to and leaving the winery or bar. It's not worth the risk. Getting home safe (and keeping others around you safe) should always be the top priority when alcohol is concerned.

Wine 101 for Beginners

What is wine? It is an alcoholic beverage that is made from fermented grape juice.

Table grapes vs. wine grapes: Table grapes are bigger and crunchier on the outside and have no seeds. Whereas wine grapes are smaller, have thicker skins, and have seeds.

Five main types of wine

Red wine—These wines range from having light to bold flavors, and they are made with black grapes. Some of the most common varieties of red wine include Cabernet Sauvignon, Cabernet Franc, Syrah, Merlot, Malbec, and Pinot Noir. No matter the variety, red wine should be served at room temperature or just below.

White wine—These wines typically range from light to rich and are made with white or (occasionally) black grapes. Common varieties include Sauvignon Blanc, Chardonnay, Riesling, and Pinot Gris or Pinot Grigio. White wines taste best at room temperature, but some people prefer them chilled.

Rosé wine—These wines are made from black grapes that are produced by removing the skins before they taint the wine deep red. However, rosé can also be made by blending red and white wine together. Both dry and sweet varieties of rosé are popular. Rosé should be chilled for thirty minutes to three hours before being served—but overchilling can affect the taste.

Sparking wine—These wines can be red, white, or rosé and range from lean to dry and rich to sweet. The bubbles are made during a second fermentation of the winemaking process. Sparkling wine should be stored in a cool and dry place and should be put on ice for around thirty minutes before serving.

Dessert wine—These wines are mostly sweet, but some are dry, and the process of making them involves fortifying the wine with spirits.

How do you taste wine?

Step 1: Take a look at the bottle to see what type of grape was used to make it and how old it is.

Step 2: Pick the right glassware (the bartender can help you if you're unsure...but depending on where you go, some places also just use universal glasses).

Step 3: Make sure that you hold the glass by the stem (holding the actual cup part will distribute heat and smell to the wine from your hand and interfere with the aromas).

Step 4: Pour and swirl about one-third of the wine in the glass. This increases the amount of oxygen in the wine and intensifies the aromas.

Step 5: Sniff the glass of wine.

Step 6: Taste the wine, but only sip, and don't swallow right away. Instead, swish it around in your mouth to absorb the flavors before finally swallowing and analyzing the different flavor profiles.

If it helps, think of it as a four-step process—look, smell, taste, and think.

Make New Memories

A fulfilled life is one that has been lived well. So, if you feel like you've been in a rut or could use some energizing, make new memories. This could mean something as simple as going over to hang out with your little nieces, nephews, or cousins to splurging on the concert of an artist you've been dying to see for years.

Whatever you feel like you need to make your life feel exciting and full, just know that you likely won't find it being cooped up in your room alone.

And sometimes, this might mean putting yourself out there and inviting friends to do something. If they say no, don't take it personally, and try again with them or other friends.

Having said that, it can also be fun to go somewhere and do something with people you've never met before. But please make sure you are always in a safe environment, and always tell at least one friend or family member where you're going to be.

Host Parties

It can be a lot of work and effort, but throwing a party—whether it's for a particular occasion, like Halloween, New Year's, Friendsgiving, or for no reason at all—is a great way to get your friends and family together.

Game nights, in particular, are awesome for getting you and your loved ones into one place and having a great time together.

If you're on a budget or simply don't feel like cooking a ton of food, it isn't rude to ask every guest to bring a dish to pass. More than likely, they'll be perfectly happy to do so since you've opened your home and will need to do all of the additional things like cleaning, potentially containing pets in one room, and preparing for visitors, which they may not be willing to do in their own houses or apartments.

Like inviting friends out to dinner, it can sometimes feel daunting to request for people to come to a party you're throwing, but aside from being a good way to bring people who are already in your life together, it's also a prime opportunity to get to know new friends a little better.

So, if you've recently moved into a new city or started classes at a new school, clean your place, get some party games, buy some drinks (or make it BYOB—bring your own booze) and food, and invite some of the people around you over for a night of fun.

Try a New Dish

Similar to sampling wine, going to a restaurant you've never been to or cooking a dish you've never had can add culture and sophistication to your life.

This goes for cuisines you've already had and those that you have not. Maybe you've tried Indian food, but you've only eaten chicken tikka masala. Next time, try saag paneer or something else. On the other hand, maybe you've never felt the courage to try sushi. Find a friend or family member who loves it to take you to their favorite Japanese spot and give it a good old try.

Who knows? You might love it, and you might hate it. That's fine as long as you tried it.

This probably goes without saying, but avoid expanding your diet to things that you are allergic to. If you aren't sure if a dish has a particular ingredient that you are sensitive to, feel free to call the restaurant or ask the server.

Take a Vacation

Whether you want to travel to another city within your state, travel across the country, or want to go abroad, taking time away from your everyday life is a great way to center yourself, relax, and gain a new perspective from people who may live very differently than you do.

However, sometimes a "staycation" (either a vacation from work where you stay home or when you rent a hotel room in the city where you live) can also be just the ticket.

Either way, taking a break from the grind of everyday life is necessary for just about everyone from time to time. So, if you feel like you could benefit from that, and your job or time in school allows for it, book that trip or just stay home. The goal is to rest if you need to rest *or* to get new experiences that you'll take with you for the rest of your life—if that's what you're interested in.

Ten Tips for Planning a Staycation

To some, the idea of just taking time off of work and staying home seems pointless and boring. But it can be anything but!

1. Get out your "fancy" sheets (if you're going to be staying home, you might as well enjoy all of the luxury you can get).

2. Add a vase of fresh flowers to your kitchen.

3. Put books that you've been meaning to read on your nightstand for the constant reminder and easy access to them.

4. Live in your robe, yoga, pants, and flip-flops (you're on

vacation...act like it!).

5. Don't turn on the news as much as you can.

6. Play relaxing music in the background.

7. Explore your city.

8. Spend as much time outside as you can.

9. Camp out in your backyard.

10. Go out for a special meal or have it delivered.

With all of the money you're saving by staying put and where you live, you should not avoid spending some money to make your time at home as luxurious, relaxing, and fun as possible.

Seven Tips for Traveling to Another City or State

Even if you are staying within your home country and are instead going to a different city, province, or area, there are several considerations you should take to keep you and your family safe.

1. **Do your research.** No matter how well you think you may know the area, double-checking that you have as much information as possible is never a bad idea.

2. **Don't draw attention.** When you're traveling, obvious signs that you are not a local make you a prime candidate for theft and other crimes. In the same vein, investing in protective clothing that will make it harder for pickpockets to access your wallet and other items is also a good use of your money before traveling. Also, pause before telling too many people that you are from out of town.

3. **Make copies of important documents.** Copies of your credit cards and driver's license should be uploaded online and printed out and carried with you. These backups will help you in a bind if the originals ever go missing.

4. **Always tell your friends and family where you are.** So, before you head out, send copies of your itinerary—and if anything changes during the trip, let them know about that. You will always be safer if someone, even one person, knows where you are at all times. It doesn't matter if you're only spending a few hours at a particular location. Someone should know.

5. **Don't automatically trust public Wi-Fi.** It is your safest option to have a virtual private network (VPN) that will allow you to access the internet while traveling because hackers can use public Wi-Fi networks to steal your credit card information or Social Security number.

6. **Make sure your hotel room is safe.** Taking extra measures like locking and dead bolting your door and keeping your window shut will help keep you safe. You should also be careful when allowing strangers into your room, even if they say they work for the hotel. In that case, call the front desk and inquire if a staff member was supposed to come to your room. And if you can, get the employee's name and see if someone that works there called. Moreover, making it look like you're in your room even when you aren't—by putting the do not disturb sign on the door and keeping the shades of the window open—can also help keep your belongings safe.

7. **Always be aware of your surroundings.** Do not fall into the trap of catching that perfect selfie for your social media.

Always keep your attention on your things and the people around you. This is not to say that you shouldn't enjoy the surroundings and experiences, but you need to trust your gut when traveling. If there's someone acting suspiciously around you or just making you uncomfortable, move away from them.

At the end of the day, when you are traveling somewhere new, being alert and on guard will only help you and your belongings make it home safely.

Ten Tips for Traveling Abroad

Traveling to another country is typically a very detailed and strict process. So, preparation before and general knowledge during your time in another country is very important.

1. **Prepare your travel documents well in advance.** The time in which you can receive your first or an updated passport can take months. And some countries won't even let you in if your passport does not have at least six months of validity left on it. So, making sure that you have plenty of time on your passport's "life" is critical, and the best time to make sure you have a valid passport is when you book your flight. If you wait until after that, the process to get a new one may delay your trip. Almost all of the same can be said for any visas that you need to get. Depending on your citizenship and the length of your stay, you may not need to apply for one, and some countries allow you to apply for one after you have already arrived, but you need to have all of that sorted well in advance.

2. **Do your research.** Look up anything you can online about

your destination, but better yet, if you can find someone who has already been, ask them everything about their experiences there. You'll want to get an overall picture of where you are going, what the people are like, if you can drink the water, what the top destinations are, what potential issues are that you'll have to deal with, and laws that you'll need to follow—despite their absurdity to you and your culture (example—it is illegal to chew gum in Singapore).

3. **Address money matters.** Before you fly over to your destination, you'll need to alert your bank that you're going to be traveling. If you do not, as soon as you try to use your credit and debit cards, they will suspect fraud. Further, knowing about the money culture in the country you're going to is also important—it's hard to access ATMs and even impossible due to a lack of card readers to use anything other than cash in some places.

4. **Be prepared for how you're going to travel once there.** Fortunately, if you're in a more developed area, rideshare apps like Uber can be easily accessible to you. But if you're tight on cash or want to live more like the locals do, planning out how to use subways and trains may be in your best interest.

5. **Book everything in advance.** You will get the most out of your trip and avoid unnecessary stress while traveling abroad by planning and paying for everything you can ahead of time. Aside from the stress element, this will also make it possible for you to have an itinerary that you can distribute to your loved ones.

6. **Avoid travel fatigue.** Instead of planning to see how many cities you can visit in one area, pause and pencil in some time to just rest. International flights are often long, stressful, and tiring. So, it takes some time to readjust. Not to mention the fact that you might be in a completely different time zone than you're used to. This often makes people feel disoriented. Furthermore, severe changes in climate have been known to make travelers physically sick with nausea or fever. Regardless of what time or climate adjustments you're dealing with during your travels, make sure you allow your body the time to process them before you head out on your adventures. If you don't, you won't enjoy them nearly as much as you would if you could fully experience them without being tired or feeling ill.

7. **Prioritize your health and safety.** This is similar to the last tip, but other than allowing a grace period for recovery from jet lag and climate changes, you should also take care to make sure that your body and belongings are safe from pickpockets, that you're connected to family and friends back home, and using your common sense at all times. In terms of common sense, do not allow yourself to be in vulnerable positions while traveling—that is, never go out at night alone, never drink so much that someone could take advantage of you, always meet new people in public areas, and just trust your gut. Another great safety hack is to purchase travel insurance to cover the items you bring with you in case your luggage gets lost or if you need to make an emergency evacuation from the country.

8. **Pack efficiently.** When preparing for your trip, think about under-packing rather than over, only bring the essentials, make sure you know what's legally allowed to fly in your

luggage and in your carry-ons, make sure you know and are abiding by the weight requirements of your airline(s), and do all that you can to keep your possessions safe en route and back.

9. **Make sure you're ready for the airport before you leave.** Ensure that you have plenty of copies of your necessary documents. Furthermore, planning ahead by knowing your terminals and how far apart they are from each other, checking in online, downloading plenty of your favorite shows and movies, and weighing your bags are all ways you can prepare for your time in the airport.

10. **Prepare ahead to connect with loved ones back home.** Especially if you are going to be traveling alone, you'll want to avoid feeling lonely or overly homesick by planning dedicated times to have video calls with your friends and family. Or if you don't want to have a call, just sharing pictures with them can also help—and they'll likely appreciate sharing in on the experience.

It can seem tedious, but preparing for an international trip is another way of loving yourself because you'll be saving unduly stress, confusion, and anxiety!

Chapter Four

Count Your Blessings

Have you ever heard the saying that instead of sheep, you should count your blessings before you fall asleep each night?

Whether you feel like it or not, more than likely, your life is filled with many great and wonderful things. But with all of the negativity on the news and social media and just in the world in general, it can be hard to appreciate them.

But considering all of the things and being grateful for all you have in your life that actually helps you live is something you should do on a regular basis if you need a reminder of just how blessed you really are. And when you feel blessed, you will probably also feel loved—by yourself for taking the time to recognize how fortunate you are and by others who help support you.

Think about this—do you have running, drinkable water in your house? If the answer is yes, you have access to something that many don't. What about a reliable ceiling over your head that keeps you safe from the elements? If yes, you also have something that many people don't. See? It's even the little things like that that most take for granted, and those are the things you should try to think about instead of spiraling about how bad your life may be.

But whether they're big or small, we're going to dive into activities you can engage in to bring the positives in your life to the forefront of your mind.

Write a Happiness List

Take time every day, every week, every month, or however frequently you want to do it, and just sit and consider all of the things in your life that make you happy. Again, they can be tiny things like seeing your cat with their best *Puss in Boots* eyes begging for breakfast when you open your eyes every morning or watching your favorite commercial on the TV. And they can be bigger things like having your significant other or best friend in your life.

Just carve out a chunk of time to truly exhaust each and every single thing around you (and about you) that makes you feel joy.

If you need inspiration, here are some small, simple things that might make you happy:

- Seeing snow falling

- Playing video games

- Visiting your grandma, who you're so blessed to still have around

- Listening to your favorite music

- Seeing your kids smile

- Sitting down with a good book

50 WAYS TO LOVE YOURSELF

- Taking ownership of your mental health
- Taking a nap
- Passing down a family recipe to a younger generation
- Enjoying a beer or cocktail (or mocktail)
- Being the giver or receiver of a random act of kindness
- Giving the perfect Christmas or birthday gift to someone you love
- Sending out thank you cards (for specific reasons—like after bridal and baby showers or just because!)
- Hearing the ice cream truck coming down the street
- Being in a location that is near a body of water
- Purging things from your home and donating them
- Hearing good news about yourself or others
- Looking through old photo albums
- Saving money for your future
- Showing your children where you grew up
- Making vision boards
- Watching your children accomplish something new for the first time
- Advocating for someone who is not in a position to stick up for themselves

- Introducing your children to your favorite hobbies
- Taking a bubble bath
- Drinking tea, coffee, or whatever, in your favorite mug
- Taking road trips
- Writing a list of things that you're grateful for
- Going out with friends
- Seeing the seasons change
- Being complimented on your looks or fashion sense
- Reciting positive affirmations
- Having an advent calendar to count down to Christmas every year
- Wrapping a warm towel around you after a shower
- Baking cookies

Whatever it is that makes you happy, make sure that you either create that experience for yourself or take the time to enjoy it when the things that are out of your control occur around you.

Explore New Cultures

Immersing yourself in another culture will not only teach you about the ways in which other people live their lives, but it will also likely make you appreciate your own culture and beliefs.

There are countless countries, regions within countries, ethnicities, and religions in the world that you can explore and educate yourself about.

If you feel like you could use some help in getting inspired, you can buy a globe or just Google world map on your laptop, then close your eyes and point at it. Wherever your finger lands, get on the internet and research everything about that place—the people, the religions, the dialects, the food.

On top of that, it could be a fun challenge to pull up some recipes from that part of the world and try to make them throughout the week or something.

But make sure that you record the places you've covered, so you can see how much you've learned and experienced throughout the journey.

This could be a very good activity to engage in with young children to help them gain new experiences they wouldn't have any other way and learn about other cultures.

However, if you are actually traveling somewhere, here are some ways in which you can learn about more about the local culture:

- Learn the language

- Research the local customs and traditions

- Venture beyond the typical tourist attractions (if it's safe to do so)

- Take public transport

- Work or volunteer abroad

- Indulge in the local food and drink

- Engage in the art scene
- Strike up conversation with the locals (again, if it's safe to do so)

Make New Traditions

If you are like most people, you've probably carried on traditions that were established when you were a child with your parents or guardians and siblings, and that's totally fine. But don't be afraid to start some new ones of your own—whether you just live by yourself, have a partner, or have children.

And they can revolve around just about anything. Maybe you want to have a nice dinner every Sunday night, or you want to incorporate an element you've heard from others around a particular holiday. Whatever it is, if it makes you smile and have good feelings around it, make it yours.

This is another area in which you can really immerse yourself in different cultures and religions. For example, if you celebrate Christmas, maybe take some time out from the holiday season to talk to someone who is Jewish or look online and learn more about the traditions associated with Hannukah. Similarly, you can learn about Bodhi Day, which is a Buddhist holiday; Kwanzaa, which is a holiday that is predominantly celebrated in Africa; Las Posadas, which is celebrated throughout Latin America and in some European countries; and others.

Perhaps you'll be inspired to incorporate some of the traditions, or versions of them, into your own holiday celebrations each year.

However, you should also be careful not to blindly follow traditions that are outdated due to changes in society or even just the maturing of your children. Traditions should be enjoyable and fun and not make people feel like they have to go along with things that make them uncomfortable due to their age or beliefs. So, if you establish a tradition, and someone or multiple people don't want to participate, that's okay. If you can still do it yourself, great. If not…maybe it's time for a new or evolved tradition.

A great example of the sentiment discussed above is a family who had a tradition to "test" the women who were going to join the family through marriage that involved stereotypical "female" tasks—like cooking or cleaning. However, despite it being more of a light-hearted thing, one of the son's fiancées said she did not feel comfortable participating in something that she deemed to be so old-fashioned. So, after a few discussions, the family proposed to include both genders in the activity. Everyone seemed comfortable with that, so that's what the tradition became from there on out.

That's the most important thing: for traditions to be fun and something everyone looks forward to doing.

If you want some inspiration, here are a few new traditions you can add to your life:

- Having a weekly game night
- Choosing a community service activity to participate in
- Having gingerbread house decorating competitions
- Taking evening walks
- Keeping a happiness jar

- Having pizza delivered once a week
- Organizing talent shows with your family
- Reading every night with your children
- Going to a baseball game every opening day
- Walking every night with your partner
- Cooking family recipes
- Having make-your-own pizza nights
- Taking one silly selfie when on vacation
- Having barbeques on Sunday afternoons
- Going apple picking each fall
- Dressing up every Christmas Eve in matching pajamas

As you can see, you can start a tradition revolving around almost anything, whether formal or informal, on a big or small scale, and occurring daily, weekly, or annually. Plus, it can come about naturally, or you can be more intentional about it.

The benefits that will come with a new tradition will be the following:

- Creating lasting memories
- Providing children with a sense of security through continuity
- Giving all members of the family the feeling of belonging
- Helping to pass along family values, including religious

heritage and culture

- Keeping generations connected

Walk Down Memory Lane When It Makes Sense

Opening up an old photo album or watching family videos from when you were a child or just a younger adult can be really uplifting and fun if you have positive memories and associations with those times.

So, if you feel like you could use a walk down memory lane, ask your parents or guardians for such albums or footage.

And while you look at the pictures or watch the videos, you might even have memories that you forgot or just need a little egging on to come back into your mind.

Even the embarrassing stuff—like the cheesy haircut your prom date had or a picture of you as a kid in a dorky outfit—is so much fun to go back and reminisce about.

But of course, as we said, in general, if you have good feelings about these moments, then they are fun to revisit. However, you may want to think twice before doing a deep dive if you have any unresolved trauma or hard feelings about those times.

Only you know what you can and can't handle at any given moment.

Moreover, you should also feel free to discard memories, such as pictures with exes, that you would prefer not to be reminded of.

Write Yourself Letters to Open Up in the Future

How cool would it be to open a letter you wrote to yourself when you were sixteen and maybe just learned how to drive? What do you think you would've said to your older self then? What mattered most to you? College aspirations? Your friends? Your crush?

Well, you can have that exact same experience in the future if you write yourself letters now for any time of your life is to come. Maybe you want to write yourself a letter to open on your wedding night, when you have your first child, or when you're fifty.

You can also write anything to yourself that you want. You can talk about your job now, your animals, your kids, your interests, anything.

Then, when you open it, you'll be reminded of the younger, childless, or whatever version of yourself. And this is a form of loving yourself in two ways—you're thinking of your future self when you write it, and then when you read it, you'll feel love for the person you were when you wrote it.

Here are some prompts to get you started on your own "future-self" letter:

- What do you want to remember about your past and your present in the future?

- What don't you want to remember?

- What are your favorite things right now?

- How are you feeling *right now*?

- What are some of the most valuable lessons you've learned so far?

- What are the lessons that you hope to learn in the future?

- How do you think you'll be different in the future?

- What do you believe is your life's purpose? Has that ever changed?

- How do you define success? Mainly, what would have to happen in your lifetime to deem it a successful one? Or you can write down what your top five priorities in life are.

- What habits do you want to add to your life? How do you plan to do that?

- If you could tell your past self one thing, what would it be? If you could tell your future self one thing, what would it be?

- What is something you've never told anyone else?

Have a Game Night with Your Family and Friends

This was already touched upon in the previous chapter, but it deserves a spot here because just being around the ones you love is another awesome way to be reminded about the blessings in your life, which they all are.

You shouldn't take a single person who contributes positively to your life for granted, just as they should express their appreciation for you. And a game night can bring out the funniest and whackiest parts of a person, and who doesn't want to be around the ones they love when they're in such a great mood?

However, sore losers and people with fragile egos (who you should probably give this book to when you're done reading it) also exist in the world, but if you're playing with one of those kinds of people, try to raise them up as much as possible, and remind them that it's just a game that you're playing for absolutely no stakes at all. Winning and losing, at the end of the day, doesn't really mean anything. The only point is to laugh and have a good time.

And there are games you can play with your family and friends that require minimal to no additional supplies, including charades, Pictionary, celebrity, movie quotes game, hangman, would you rather, never have I ever, and twenty-one questions.

Play with Your Kids

Sometimes, your greatest blessings are hiding in plain sight, and that's sometimes exactly what happens with your children. You birthed them, you pay to meet all of their needs, and sometimes, they just wear you out with their demands and protests.

But think of it in the context that you only get seventeen summers with your kids before they are grown up—only seventeen summers. That isn't a lot of time in the grand scheme of life.

So, you'd be best advised to take advantage of every single second you have available to roll around in the grass, play a game of catch, listen to their stories that might not make sense, and just interact with your child.

There will be big moments like going to Disney World and birthdays, but there are also the little moments like snuggling on the couch at the end of a long day and watching your child's favorite movie for the thousandth time. Both are important, and you never know what memories they will keep for the rest of their lives.

So, sing along to every song, take every opportunity for tickles, and just have fun with your children. You have been blessed with being a parent, and not everyone can say that.

If you are having trouble coming up with family fun things you can do with your children, here are a few to consider:

- Start a garden or attend to an existing one
- Go on a hike
- Go roller skating (outside or in a rink)
- Develop a scavenger hunt
- Go to a museum, zoo, or aquarium
- Go to a playground
- Ride bikes around the neighborhood or on trails
- Fly a kite
- Do a puzzle
- Work on random science experiments
- Go to the water park or pool
- Blow bubbles

- Color pictures

- Ice skating

- Go outside and draw with chalk on the driveway or sidewalk

- Set up a projector in the backyard and watch a movie

- Cook or bake something

- Go to a ceramic shop and paint something

- Volunteer for the less fortunate

Recognize Your Achievements and Celebrate Them

Part of loving yourself is giving you credit where credit is due—and like so many other of these tips, this one also comes in varying degrees.

Of course, you should take time to praise yourself and celebrate the big accomplishments, like graduating from school, getting a new job, getting a promotion, breastfeeding your infant for a time you set for yourself, or having a child in the first place.

But the "small" achievements should also not go uncelebrated. That's not to say you should be boastful to others, but it's perfectly okay to acknowledge yourself for a job well done when you come home with a week's worth of food that you bought for your family, pull off a new, complicated recipe, do something that scares you like driving on the highway, or even each day when you make your bed and brush your teeth in the morning.

Those are all things you intended to achieve, and you made the choice of whether or not to actually do them.

Each day that you provide for yourself and your family in any way, shape, or form should be celebrated. You're awesome…if anyone is going to feel that way, it sure as heck better be you!

Enjoy Time at Home

Similar to spending time with your kids, you should also set some time aside to just enjoy the home that you've built for yourself and the surroundings in it that you've cultivated for your space.

This is especially true if you have animals, children, or a significant other. All of those things matter so much more than anything else that is happening in the outside world.

That's not to say you can't go to events, parties, or bars. You should feel the freedom to spend your money and your free time in any way you see fit. But just don't forget about the faces waiting for you at home.

And even if you live alone, your home is a reflection of you. You chose to purchase that particular picture or piece of art, and you chose to put that in the exact place that it is on your wall. You might want to take time and actually enjoy these things.

Moreover, if you have a good relationship with your parents and other relatives, and especially if you don't live close by or visit often, take advantage of the time that you have them around. Go back to where you grew up or wherever they live now and just visit them. You don't have to do anything else—you can simply sit down at their kitchen table and talk. You never know when they'll be gone, and when they are, you'll probably be wishing you'd gone to see them more.

If it's your goal to spend more time at home in any capacity, you can try the following:

- **Cleaning your house.** The cleaner and tidier your space is, the more time you'll likely want to spend more time inside of it (and some people avoid their homes when they're messy and unorderly).

- **Learning a new skill.** Adapting hobbies like cooking, painting, or fixing up an old car that can be done at home will also promote your time there.

- **Trying at-home workouts.** Other than intense weightlifting, almost every other kind of exercise can be done at home. And if you need inspiration, just hop online and look for yoga, cardio, or kickboxing guides.

- **Dedicating yourself to finishing a book.** Everyone has those books sitting on their shelves that are collecting dust that they have recently not cracked open. So, go ahead and make the commitment to sprawl out in your reading nook or favorite leisure spot and do some reading!

- **Catching up on or rewatching your favorite show.** This is probably one of the easier ways to pass the time at home. After cuddling into your couch, chair, or bed, turn on the TV, your phone, your laptop, or your tablet, and select a show that makes you feel good.

- **Practicing meditation and mindfulness.** Especially if you find that you are stressed at home—due to clutter, your partner, your children, your animals—adopting a consistent meditation practice will help reduce these negative feelings and make you more present for the precious time that you do spend in your house.

- **Having a spa day.** Instead of getting help from an outside professional, you can practice self-care (and have the others in your household participate) by pampering yourself with a bubble bath, hair treatment, face mask, manicure, and whatever else you feel like indulging in.

- **Taking an online class or tutorial.** Is there a skill you've always wanted to learn? Well, pull the plunge and make the commitment of taking an online course in that subject. This will serve as a productive way for you to spend more time at home.

- **Starting a journal or blog.** You can do this just for fun or in the hopes of turning it into a new career venture. Heck! You can even kill two birds with one stone and start a blog about the ways in which other moms, dads, twenty-somethings, etc., can spend more time at home.

- **Spending time with the ones you love.** While you're taking time at home, try your best to really enjoy it. Have a conversation with your partner or your kids. Take your dog out to play in the backyard.

- **Taking a social media break**. "Banning" yourself for hours or days is a great way to refocus and concentrate on your family.

Enjoy Social Events

So much of your life is spent thinking about anything else than the present. So, when you get the opportunity to go to a concert, musical, or any social outing like that that often requires an expensive ticket and dressing up, you should try to avoid thinking about yesterday, tomorrow, or any other time other than the one you're currently living in.

You probably worked hard to afford the experience, so you deserve to enjoy it to the absolute fullest that you can.

The same goes for smaller events like holiday parties, birthday parties, and random get-togethers. You should try to enjoy each and every moment you have with your friends and families. As we mentioned in the last tip, you never know how long you have people in your life for. That's not just for the older people in your life. The lives of anyone—regardless of age—can change in an instant. So, appreciating and just soaking up the time you have with them is so, so important.

This ties a couple of the other tips together with this one, but doing your best to stay present and recognizing the blessings, be it opportunities or just quality time with people who are currently present in your life, is just another way for you to show love to yourself. You are fully enjoying the moment, and you deserve that. Tomorrow can worry for itself. What's important is the here and now.

And if you find that you struggle with being present and constantly worry about the future, therapy of some kind may be able to help you with that as well as medications that your doctor can prescribe you. Whatever you need to do in order to enjoy this short life you all have on the planet, please be courageous enough to admit you need help, seek it out, and receive it without ego.

Chapter Five

Explore Your Inner Self

It makes sense that you have to know yourself in order to truly love yourself, right? But so many people don't take the time to fully delve into who they are as a person and focus more on the things that they do—that's not to say your work and hobbies are not a part of who you are, but who you are on the inside apart from those things is also very important.

In this chapter, we'll discuss ways in which you can learn more about the kind of person that you are.

Celebrate Your Emotional Strengths

Everyone is a flawed human being with their own strengths and weaknesses. But when you can acknowledge both, forgive yourself in the areas that you lack and put in the work to improve on them, and celebrate the strengths you already possess, then you are on your way to becoming an emotionally intelligent person who understands yourself (and others around you) better.

But as this book is all about loving yourself, the focus should be heavily on the side of recognizing the strengths you already have.

If you're not sure what your emotional strengths are, let's go over a few things:

- Do you feel a sense of respect and need to control yourself around people who are older? If yes, that's an emotional strength.

- Do you feel sympathy for someone you see sleeping on a bench or is otherwise struggling somehow? If yes, that's an emotional strength.

- Do you ever wonder what it would feel like to steal something, but you know you never could in a million years because it would weigh too heavy on your conscience? If yes, that's an emotional strength.

- Do you feel the need to be honest with your significant other and friends? If so, that's an emotional strength.

- Are you able to calm yourself down before exploding on someone in a stressful situation? If yes, that's an emotional strength.

- Have you ever had a friend change plans on you at the last second, and you just rolled with it? If yes, that is an emotional strength.

Basically, anything you can do to control your mood, behavior, and thoughts and make them better is what emotional strength is. So, the next time someone says an opinion that you do not agree with—like a grandparent who votes for the opposing political party—but you know that it would be inappropriate for you to say something, and you keep your mouth shut, that's emotional strength and intelligence.

Of course, that's not to say that you shouldn't voice your opinion at times. But if whatever was said is not specifically targeted at an individual or group of people around and not in a position to defend themselves, and you read the room and know that a disruption or argument would only ruin or temper the experience for everyone else around…it's probably best not to say anything.

If whatever was said was really bugging you, you can always approach the individual who said something you believe to be problematic and address it with them privately.

Understand That You're Human

One of the greatest gifts you can give yourself is the grace to be a human. And inherently, humans make mistakes. You forget things, you misplace things, you drop things, and sometimes you just flat out fall on your faces.

As long as the mistake is not life-threatening or career-ruining for you or others, instead of getting angry at yourself the next time you make one, take a deep breath in and out and remind yourself that you are a human—and humans mess up sometimes.

But with this grace also comes the responsibility of learning from your mistakes. Suppose you forgot your mom's birthday, and that really hurt her feelings. Well, next year, you better be sure that you have it down in your calendar to prevent forgetting again. Or you were a few minutes late to work because you forgot to set your alarm clock and woke up late. The next night, you should set two alarms just to be safe the following morning.

So, when you make a mistake, forgive yourself, and make a plan for what you will do differently in the same or a similar situation the next time.

What does it mean to be a human?

- A being who was born with knowledge, conscience, and free will

- A being who has moral responsibilities that other entities (like animals and plants) do not have to be held accountable for

- A being who was gifted with the ability to reason and discern

- A being who sees themselves in relation to their values, choices, and relationships with others

- A being who, despite having advanced intelligence, does not always have perfect judgment

Explore Spirituality

Whether you believe in some form of a god or you believe that the universe controls everything, it's probably safe to say that we all agree that *something* controls the world we live in.

If you're more on the religious side, you likely think about things like:

- What practices or rituals do I need to follow in order to conform to the Bible?

- What is right and what is wrong in the eyes of my god?

- What is true and what is false according to the god I follow?

But if you fall in line with being more spiritual, you likely think about things like:

- Where do I find meaning? Is it from the universe? Or somewhere else?

- What do I feel connected to? Is it the universe? Or is it something else?

- How should I live in accordance with the higher good that I believe in?

The cool thing is that contexts of religion and spirituality can overlap, and when you think about them, you are considering your beliefs, your source of comfort, the perception of the world you want to have, and your code of ethics. You're getting to know yourself.

So, if you're safe, secure, and happy in your current religion, that's great. But if you have never really felt comfortable being a part of an organized religion, you are encouraged to check the spirituality aspect out. A great place to start is by finding a quiet space and journaling about what you *truly* believe.

And you can try answering the questions above if that will help you decipher which side of the spectrum (if not both) you fall under regarding religion vs. spirituality.

Find New Hobbies

Although a hobby is technically something you do, it still says a lot about you based on the hobbies you choose. It also speaks volumes about what you want in life, depending on how you choose to do that particular hobby.

An example would be liking to shoot basketball hoops. If you are someone who likes to keep to yourself more often than being around other people, you might go shoot hoops by yourself at the local park. But if you're more extroverted or looking to make new friends, you'll probably be on the lookout for local pickup games or clubs that you can join and meet people.

Another example is crocheting. Typically, that could be seen as a very solitary hobby, but if you enjoy it and also like socializing with people who share the same hobby as you, you too can look for hobby groups that have regular meeting times for everyone to come together, crochet, and chat.

Whatever you like to do in your spare time, you should take the time to do it. And if you don't already have any hobbies or are getting tired of old ones, try something new. You'll learn a lot about yourself as you navigate and try different things—and like we've said in this book already, you don't truly know if you like something unless you try it first. Just please make sure that if it's a hobby that puts your safety at risk, take care to learn the best ways to keep your body protected by someone more seasoned in the activity.

Hobbies to consider trying include:

- Dancing.

- Photography.

- Glassblowing.

- Acting.

- Singing or playing an instrument.

- Knitting.

- Woodworking.

- Gardening.

- Creative writing.

- Winemaking or brewing beer.

- Drawing or painting.

- Pottery.

- Metalwork.

- Cooking.

- Sewing.

- Beekeeping.

- Digging into the genealogy of yourself and others.

- Computer programming.

- Geocaching.

- Video editing and many, many more!

And hobbies don't just take up your spare time. They also:

- Help you build and maintain relationships with people.

- Help you reduce your stress levels.

- Help make you a well-rounded, interesting person.

- Improve your mental health.

- Help you learn new skills (which you may be able to use in a career change…if that's what you want).

- Offer you new challenges.

- Improve your memory.

- Help you improve and hold onto fine motor skills and hand-eye coordination.

- Make your life more fun.

Become Your Own Best Friend

Especially when you're engaging in self-talk about the way you look—the way your nose looks, the way your teeth look when you smile, your weight, anything—please make an effort to stop yourself and question, "Would I talk to my best friend like this?"

If you're a decent human, you'll likely answer no.

Then, think about how you speak to your actual best friend. You're usually encouraging, understanding, and empathetic. Right?

So, if you can be that for someone else, why can't you also be that for yourself? When you look in the mirror, point out the things that you like and tell yourself that you are beautiful. Because you know what? You are! As long as you are someone who contributes positively to this world and the collective consciousness, you are beautiful on the inside and out.

In summary, in all the ways that you are there for your best friend, you should also provide that same support to yourself. That means complimenting yourself, being understanding of yourself when life gets tough and you just need a good cry, and overall just showing up for yourself. Be your own number-one advocate!

This can be a hard concept to wrap your mind around, but be patient. You are actually in the perfect position to know the support and assistance you require...you just need to give it to yourself.

None of this is to implicate that you shouldn't have external friendships. It's simply saying that in addition to them, you should be your own ride-or-die first.

Some tips on how to be your own best friend:

1. When you look in the mirror, try to remind yourself that there never has been, and there never will be, another you!

2. When you talk to yourself, be kind.

3. Try getting into the habit of thinking about positive affirmations. For example, say, "I'm enough," "I'm worthy of love," "I deserve to be successful." Hone in on the things you want in your life and develop your mantras from there (and they will change).

4. Don't be afraid to give yourself a hug when you need it...that might sound crazy, but don't knock it until you try it!

5. Schedule times to check in with yourself. Just like you'd send your friend a text asking how they are, do the same for yourself.

6. Seek inspiration to be a more positive being from internal sources (from yourself) rather than from the external.

7. Give yourself approval rather than wait for someone to give it to you.

8. Stand up for yourself.

9. Only surround yourself with people who love you and respect you.

10. Listen and tend to your own needs.

11. Write out a list of all of your strengths.

12. Buy yourself a nice gift from time to time.

13. Remember that it isn't selfish to spend time alone when you need it.

When it comes down to it, the biggest part about being your own friend is being kind and supportive to and loving of yourself. This can be a hard habit to maintain, but it will only get easier with practice!

Chapter Six

Boundaries

We've already touched a bit on the importance of setting boundaries around yourself when it comes to friends, family members, and just about anyone else in your life.

But this is such an important concept that it also deserves its own chapter. So, here are a few ways in which you can set firmer boundaries in your life. (Remember, only someone who loves themselves will put them first in any given relationship.)

Set Boundaries for the People in Your Life

When it comes to anybody in your life, it's up to you how much access they have to you. Say you have a friend who comes over and always overstays their welcome, but outside of that, they are actually a good friend. It's okay to stop inviting them to your place and instead ask them to go for coffee dates or something that requires going to another establishment or location. And you don't even have to tell that friend why you're doing it. You can, if you feel like it's necessary, but if not, even if the friend asks to come over, suggest going out for lunch or something instead.

Or suppose it's something more serious, and you felt that your mother emotionally neglected you as a child. Now, as you're both adults, she leans on you to be her "emotional-support daughter." But after everything she didn't do for you, if you don't feel the obligation to do that, you are well within your right to distance yourself from your mother.

But unlike the friend example, you should probably tell your mom that you're not open to hearing her vent about the troubles in her life, and it's because of the way she treated you growing up. She may protest or become upset, but stand your ground. Your feelings are valid. And if you don't feel the responsibility of caring for your mother in that way, that's okay.

Another area in life where people need to set boundaries for themselves is in the workplace. Unfortunately, there isn't a whole lot outside of the requirements set by the law—like protection from sexual harassment—that you can limit in terms of things your boss asks you to do within the workday. However, if you work in a profession that does not require immediate attention and emails can wait to be opened the next business day or after the weekend, you can set the rule for yourself that you do not answer work emails at night or on the weekends.

The only thing with that, again, is that it depends on your profession. Some issues need to be resolved right away, so it really matters what you actually do for a living. But if you can make that rule, you need to hold to it because the minute you break it, you will be telling your boss that it is a flimsy boundary, and they will likely expect you to break it more often.

Of course, if it's project-specific, and you absolutely have to break it, that's fine. But make sure you are only doing so because of the pressing nature of that project.

Have Consequences in Mind and Stick to Them

When you set a boundary, in order to make sure you keep it in place, it's best to imagine what the consequence will be if you do break it.

For example, the mother problem we just talked about: for a child to set the boundary that they will not be their mother's emotional support, they need to keep strong to do that and realize that the consequence of caving, even once, will mean that they're telling her it's okay to call them and rant for hours on end. And in doing so, that child may feel like the mother is not experiencing the justice she deserves for emotionally neglecting her child.

Just like we mentioned in the work boundaries example—the consequence of answering an email at night or on the weekend when you told yourself you would not do that would be to communicate to your boss that you are open to working during those times when you'd rather be spending with family.

Whenever you set a boundary, do not do so lightly, and anytime you feel like breaking it, just remember the consequences that you very likely will face if you break it.

Once you show people they can walk all over you, they tend to do it and take full advantage.

Don't Overshare

This is especially difficult in the age of social media that we are currently in, and it's your instinct to post about every aspect of your life. But you will only benefit yourself from taking a beat after pressing "post" and reflecting on whether or not the cyber world truly needs to know about whatever you just typed or have pictured.

Now, if it's something impersonal, like a picture of you at the state fair, that's probably fine. But when it comes to intimate details about your family, friend groups, or relationship, you should put a very strict boundary about not oversharing that with people...and sometimes people you don't even know in real life. You don't want those people who you don't know to gain access to enough information to deceive you that they know a family member of yours and have been told things about you from them.

In general, here are some things you should avoid sharing online:

- Complaints about work or private company information
- Your banking information
- Too many drinking photos (some are fine...a lot can be concerning)
- Photos of people without their permission
- Pictures of your children that they might find embarrassing in the future
- Exact travel plans (or skip posting altogether before you return home)
- Self-incriminating evidence of any kind

- Expensive new purchases

- Your location

- Your child's school

- Hate speech toward anyone or anything

- Your personal address

But you should also be careful not to overshare with people in person either. Never underestimate how much people like to gossip, and unless the person you're speaking with has proven to you that they are trustworthy, do not tell them anything you wouldn't want someone else to find out about you, another friend, a significant other, or a family member.

In general, it's best to keep a small group of friends—even if that's just one single person—who you know will keep your secrets...however, you should probably only share *your* secrets. You don't want to be the person that always airs other people's business.

And if you don't have one good friend like that, hopefully you have a sister, cousin, aunt, or other relative who you can go to. But also remember, there are people called therapists that you can pay to listen to all of your grievances and even give you educated feedback.

You may often also feel the desire to overshare with your family. Sometimes, that's prompted by you or sometimes by them when they ask about areas of your life that were appropriate for them to know about when you were a child but not anymore.

The best example of that is when it comes to money. Unless you need help, the only people who truly need to know about your financial situation is you, anyone with whom you share something like rent and bills, and anyone who cosigns a loan with you. That's it. If none of those people are your family, then they don't need to know. However, if they are trustworthy, you should not hesitate to contact them if you need help with money management or other financial situations.

Practice Forgiveness

Similar to giving yourself the grace of being a human who messes up sometimes, you also need to be able to forgive yourself. That means forgiving yourself for mistakes you've made in the past, and that includes versions of yourself that you have done the work to move on and improve from.

You cannot change the past, and dwelling on things you've already done, barring if you seriously injured or caused damage to someone, is typically a waste of time. All you can really control is what you're doing now and what you do in the future.

Just as you'd be willing to forgive your partner, friend, or family member for messing up from time to time, you also need to forgive yourself, and sometimes that's as easy as just letting things go. However, make sure you learn a lesson from each mistake.

You said something mean to someone when you were in high school that you'd never dream of saying today...forgive yourself and let it go. You've already done the work because you're now someone who wouldn't talk like that. And the person you said it to probably doesn't remember anyway, but if it would make you feel better, apologize to them as well if you can get in contact with them.

You made a very stupid decision and had a little too much to drink and drove your car. Well, first of all, thank your lucky stars you didn't kill yourself or anyone else, and then forgive yourself for doing that. Then, promise that you will absolutely never risk doing that again, and let the mistake (not the promise) go.

In the end, everyone falls flat sometimes, and all you can do is pick yourself up, learn how to avoid that mistake in the future (if possible), and move on with your life.

If you need to forgive yourself for something you did in the past, this book should serve as a sign that it's time to let that go, so you can instead focus on being the very best version of yourself. Dwelling on the past only keeps you from that.

But don't confuse self-forgiveness for self-compassion. They are not the same things. Self-compassion is more like self-care, and it requires you to be kind to yourself when you experience setbacks, recognize that you are not the only person in the world who struggles from time to time, and have the clarity and mindfulness to recognize when they are having negative thoughts.

Strategies for self-forgiveness include:

- **Thinking back**—remember a time in your life—whether from childhood or more recent—when you felt cared for. Then, think about who was caring for you. It can be a parent, friend, teacher, or even a pet. After that, picture that that person or animal is in the room with you, and together with them, write down all of your positive qualities.

- **Remembering the event**—think about all of the facts surrounding the specific event you feel like you need to forgive yourself for. Do not be afraid to face the parts that are hard to face. That's all part of the experience. And you'll want to eventually sort the facts into three categories:

moral faults (things you feel guilty or ashamed for doing), unskillfulness (things you promise to never do again), and everything else.

- **Not avoiding guilt**—it's actually a very good sign if you feel guilt or shame over what you need to forgive yourself for. That indicates that you are a good person. Bad people do bad things and feel nothing. Also, feeling guilty can make you accountable for not repeating the same behavior in the future.

- **Taking responsibility**—you cannot fully forgive yourself until you acknowledge what you did wrong to yourself and the person(s) who you may have hurt. It's easy for people to push certain details far away into their minds in order to avoid guilt. But remember, that isn't fully owning up to what you did, and you can't forgive what you don't acknowledge.

Don't think of it as self-indulgent—some may believe that going through the process of forgiving yourself is a self-serving thing, but when done correctly, it's actually more of a weighing of your capacity for doing good or bad.

Don't Forget "You" Time

Setting time aside for yourself, and yourself alone, gets especially tricky as you become an adult with a job, a partner, children, and pets. But it's so important for your mental health and well-being that you prioritize yourself from time to time.

Maybe that means going on a long walk, going for a drive, watching your favorite show by yourself, going to a movie alone, or anything else that you enjoy doing that can be done with only you.

This will benefit not only you but also your entire family. If you're more relaxed, you're less likely to snap or otherwise react negatively about the little things that don't actually have a big consequence.

Taking time for yourself is also a boundary that you cannot waver on. Moreover, if a situation arises in your life, like your spouse, child, or parent falling ill, and there's no one available to care for them, you can still find times, like when they are asleep, to sneak in the solitary time you need.

Please also be aware that based on your personality type, you might require more or less personal time. Whatever you need and can reasonably take without falling behind on your personal, work, and financial responsibilities is perfectly fine for you. And if you feel like you need more than your current responsibilities are allowing, talk to someone about that—your spouse, your boss, or whoever is in control or in a place to lessen your load in some way.

The change may feel less daunting if you present it as an issue that might resolve itself with time, but if it doesn't, that's okay too. Burnout in your profession and just life in general is a real thing, and it should be prevented at all costs! It's better to get ahead of things and circumvent going through that turmoil in the first place. Remember, be your best advocate!

Here are twelve ways to find more "you" time in your day:

1. **Examine your attitude around time management and take ownership of your schedule.** Planning out your day in increments can help you stay prioritized on the things that need to be done now. Then, you may find that you have an extra hour or two at the end of the night.

2. **Analyze how you spend your time.** Developing a time log can help you manage your time and see what time you may be wasting.

3. **Divide your time into quadrants.** This is especially helpful if you find long to-do lists daunting. Start by dividing your time into four quadrants as so:

   Quadrant one is for important and urgent matters (for instance, paying bills, getting ready for work on time).

   Quadrant two is for important and nonurgent matters (for instance, spending time with your kids, friends, and other loved ones who matter to you).

   Quadrant three is for unimportant and urgent matters (for instance, answering when your mother calls you or getting a package off of your front porch when it arrives).

   Quadrant four is for unimportant and nonurgent (for instance, watching YouTube videos or going on social media).

4. **Plan your day beforehand.** When it comes to organizing your time, it can be helpful for some to plan for the day ahead on the night before. Further, completing one big task right away in the morning can help you gain the momentum you need to be productive for the rest of the day.

5. **Limit interruptions.** If you are working on a time-sensitive project, you can limit distractions by silencing your phone, avoiding your email, and putting capped time limits on your social media time.

6. **Abide by the two-minute rule.** If a task on your to-do list for the day will take two minutes and another will take several hours, do the two-minute one first.

7. **Do not procrastinate.** Continue to be active and on top of your tasks at hand. Avoiding things will only bring you more headaches down the road. Plus, it feels so good to be productive!

8. **Prioritize "big" tasks.** We don't necessarily mean big in circumstance. For example, making your bed can have the most impact on the look of your room. Another task of this nature is doing the dishes. It can make your kitchen look less cluttered and cleaner.

9. **Know yourself and how quickly you can do certain things.** If you're working on a project that is going to take a large chunk of time, divvy it up into pieces, so that you can have small breaks. This will help avoid burnout and unnecessary stress. Moreover, you should also evaluate when in the day you have the most energy and focus—for some people, this is right away in the morning, for others, it's late at night.

10. **Plan to be at least fifteen minutes early to work, meetings, and other engagements.** By planning to be early, you are more likely to be on time if there are obstacles along your way, such as accidents, construction, or anything else that can hold you up on the road.

11. **Prepare as much as you can ahead of time.** When it comes to work, packing your lunch and briefcase beforehand will save you time in the morning and help you get to the office in time.

12. **Know that it's okay to leave some things unfinished.** If something does not need to be done today due to deadlines or other requirements, leave it on the to-do list for another day in favor of having some leisure time if you need it.

By using these planning mechanisms, hopefully, you'll find gaps in the day where you can enjoy time to yourself that you would've otherwise just wasted by procrastinating on something that needs to be done, doing something that isn't even urgent in the first place, or anything other than an activity you like doing.

Chapter Seven

Remain Grounded in Yourself While You Grow

The thing about learning more about who you are is that you never stop doing so. You're constantly evolving and changing your opinion, or at least you should be.

There are several things you can do in life to help you do this, and we'll discuss some of those in this chapter.

Be a Mentor

A great way to give back to your community is by becoming a mentor to someone. Sometimes, this relationship comes about naturally in life, or you can get the ball rolling if it doesn't by enrolling in programs like Big Sisters and Big Brothers.

Whatever way you go about finding someone who can benefit from you taking them under your wing, please be aware that they are helping fill a need in you as much as you're doing that for them. If you have the desire to become a mentor for someone, doing just that is fulfilling a desire for or lack of something that you clearly need in your life. So, expect to learn just as much from your mentee, and you plan to teach them too.

However, you can also just be a great mentor in life by being the best person you can possibly be. Those around you will notice, and if they admire something about you and your life, they'll model themselves after you. That's probably the best way to mentor someone if you don't have the time to actually meet up and be there for one or more specific people.

Aside from the ways already mentioned, you can also be a mentor by participating in the following activities:

- Allowing someone to shadow you at your job.

- Volunteering to serve on a panel at local colleges (like mock trials and other presentations).

- Join an organization that will match you up with a child to be pen pals with.

- Participate in reverse mentoring, which flips things on its head, and if you are the senior employee, you will actually be the one being mentored by a junior employee (or vice versa if you're the junior employee).

- Become a peer mentor for someone who is also a student at your school or who holds a similar amount of responsibility at your work.

- Look into identity mentoring, which includes the mentor and mentee being part of a group of people (mothers, female entrepreneurs) or being a mentor to a mentee who is curious about a group you are part of (LGBTQIA+, veterans).

But if you are planning on establishing a long-term, one-on-one mentorship with someone, there are a few things you should consider and question several things before and during the relationship, including:

- Understanding what each party wants out of your time together

    - Is this a two-way street? Meaning, are you going to learn from one another? Or are you looking for something else?

- Setting the expectations together at the very beginning

    - Is there a timeline for when the mentorship ends?

    - How often should you meet and why?

    - What kind of resources would the mentee like to receive from the mentor?

    - How are you going to measure the success of the mentorship?

    - How hands-on does the mentee want the mentor to be? And how involved does the mentor want to be?

- Taking a genuine interest in your mentee

    - Are you open and prepared to take an interest in the things that they like to do?

- Taking the time to build mutual trust

- Knowing when it's appropriate for you to give advice

- Not assuming anything about your mentee

- The necessity of sharing your journey together

  - Are you ready to be vulnerable enough to cope with your previous, current, and projected struggles? If so, your mentee will likely feel more comfortable opening up to you about your own.

- Celebrating their achievements

  - Ask your mentee what their love language is. Depending on what it is—obviously, physical touch (unless it's a hug, and the two of you have both communicated that that is okay) is mostly inappropriate—you can rely on that to guide you on how to celebrate these.

- Seeking out resources to help your mentee grow

- Ensuring that you have the bandwidth to take on a mentee

  - Do you think of mentoring someone as a task or a calling? Hopefully, you'll answer the latter.

  - Do you really have the time to be mentoring someone? It's okay to say no.

  - Are you willing and open to dealing with someone who may have had or is having a troubled upbringing? Depending on the program you go through, if at all, you might be tasked with working with a mentee who has had their fair share of trauma, and if you cannot see yourself hearing about it, you may want to reconsider mentoring someone because rejection over trauma just creates more trauma.

Clear the Clutter

Sometimes, all that is standing in the way of you and your self-confidence is a tidy home. So, take the time to love yourself and your space and clean it up.

Speaking of love, if you find that you just have too much stuff, pick each individual item—be it clothing, fragrances, dishes, anything—and determine if they make you feel lovingly toward it. If not, it's probably time for it to find another home.

It could also be a boundary you set for yourself that you will not let your house get dirty and cluttered like this again. This way, you're going to establish a schedule to pick up throughout the week instead of letting everything pile up on top of each other in order to make keeping your space clean easier.

Then, with a clean house, maybe you'll feel more comfortable inviting friends and family over. So, if that's a goal for you, that would be a wonderful set of boundaries to start making for yourself.

Please also don't be afraid to reach out for help if you're overwhelmed by your clutter. Check online to see if there are any services you can pay for or even volunteer services that could come in and help you.

Further, if you feel like it's difficult to let go of anything, including things that should not hold sentimental value to you, such as cables, paper plates, meat trays, therapy might be a good avenue for you to explore. But do not be ashamed if you need help. We all do in one area of our life or the other.

If you need the motivation, here are some reasons to declutter your home:

- It will look cleaner, and you will have less to clean in preparation for guests.

- When you are organized, it makes things much easier to find.

- You'll likely feel less stressed.

- Once you eliminate the number of things you own, you need to keep things that way. So, without buying unnecessary things that will just sit around without being used, you'll end up saving money. This can allow you to gain financial freedom.

- When you have a clean house, it makes it easier to motivate yourself to keep it clean.

- Without the need to dedicate an entire day to cleaning, you will have more time for your passion projects.

And here are ten decluttering tips that you can choose to follow:

1. If you're just starting your decluttering journey, take things slow and try doing five minutes of cleaning at a time.

2. In that same vein, you can also start by giving just one thing away.

50 WAYS TO LOVE YOURSELF

3. Once you get comfortable with purging, make it a goal to fill an entire garbage bag full of stuff to give away.

4. Go through your closet and throw away any clothes that you haven't worn in the last six months or a year. If you need help determining this, you can hang the clothes you put back into your closet facing the wrong direction. Then, at the end of the time you deem fit to purge, you'll clearly be able to see what clothes are still facing the right way—and then you'll know to get rid of those.

5. Create a checklist of areas to tackle. This will help motivate you to get started but also give you the satisfaction of crossing things off once you go through that area of your house.

6. Try the twelve-twelve-twelve challenge. This involves finding twelve items to donate, twelve items to throw away, and twelve items to be given away to somebody. In the end, you'll have thirty-six things out of your home.

7. Try to view your home as a first-time visitor. Write down what your first impression would be if you were and how clean you'd determine it to be.

8. Take a before and after photo of an area of your home. Like crossing things off of a checklist, this is also a satisfying way to view your progress.

9. Don't hesitate to ask for help. You can always ask a good friend or family member to go through your home and make suggestions about things that can be thrown away.

10. Try the four-box method. Get four boxes and label them as trash, give away, keep, or relocate. Then, go through every

room in your home and evaluate every single item inside of it. It's important not to skip anything because this will give you an idea of what you actually own and what you do with it.

Volunteer

Part of being a great mentor and member of the community is by volunteering, and there is just about every opportunity to do so as you could imagine, and they include the following:

- **Animal shelters**—you can donate your spare time to playing with kittens and puppies, cleaning enclosures, transporting animals from one place to another, or doing anything else the shelter might need.

- **Fostering animals**—it takes just a few classes for you to be certified by a shelter to be able to foster animals. And after doing that, you will be on the list of volunteers that take animals into your home until they are adopted. This clears room in the shelters for even more animals. Aside from the time and money you have to spend, it will also likely be hard for you to part with the animal if they have been with you for a while, but remember that the goal of fostering is for you to eventually say goodbye because that means you can help even more animals.

- **Politics**—you can volunteer to be a poll worker, assist in voter registration, or give your time specifically to a candidate you feel is most qualified—that may involve cold calling or petitioning.

- **Hospitals**—you can volunteer to do skin-to-skin at your local hospital for newborns whose mothers are not able to provide that to them. Or you can do your part to entertain the patients during the stressful time of being hospitalized by playing an instrument or singing.

- **Building**—you can volunteer to build homes for families in need.

- **Coaching**—you can coach a soccer, football, baseball, dance, cheerleading, or other sports team, and that's a form of volunteering.

- **Mentoring**—as we discussed already, you can become a mentor for someone and agree to regular hangouts and to help your mentee in any area of life they might need it.

- **Blood centers**—you can donate by giving your blood or platelets to help someone in need of a transfusion.

- **Assisted living and nursing homes**—at any time or just around the holidays, you can volunteer to spend time with older people who may not have a family or friends of their own.

- **Libraries**—many libraries rely on volunteers to help their overall operation.

- **Homeless shelters**—like libraries, homeless shelters benefit heavily from the work of volunteers who come in to prepare and serve food and do other tasks around the shelter.

- **Tutoring**—you can volunteer to help students at any level to improve their skills in a given subject. This can be done in person or virtually.

- **Cleaning up**—you can get in contact with your city and let them know that you are interested in joining a clean-up crew to help improve the look of where you live. This will often involve going outside and picking up trash from the side of the road.

- **Donating**—the simple act of donating items that no longer serve you is also a form of volunteering.

- **Becoming a board member**—if you find a nonprofit that you really like and support, you can become a board member, which is often an unpaid position you take to help make certain decisions on behalf of the organization.

- **Teaching a skill**—if you are talented at doing something, be it coding, playing the piano, or woodworking, you can reach out to your local youth centers and see if they'd be interested in having you come and teach a workshop to the often-underserved children who frequent their facility.

- **Making clothing and blankets**—if you like to crochet, knit, or sew, you can use your free time to make clothing and blankets for people who are experiencing homelessness and animals who are in shelters. You'll enjoy the process of making the item, and then someone will benefit from receiving it.

- **Translator**—people who speak sign and foreign languages can serve different organizations by translating for people who are not fluent in English.

- **Being a friend**—there are programs (like Best Buddies) that will pair you up with an adult who experiences intellectual and developmental disabilities, and you will simply be their friend. This improves the lives of both people involved and promotes inclusion for a group of people who have so often been excluded.

Essentially, every way in which you can help your community or someone in particular, and you are not receiving monetary compensation for that time, you are volunteering. And the ones mentioned are just a few of the things you can volunteer your time and effort for. There are an unlimited number of other ways you can give back. And by helping others, you're feeling good about yourself (which is a form of love!).

Revisit Places of Significance

If you feel like you could use a pick-me-up, going back to places that are special to you can help a great deal. Chalk it up to nostalgia, the placebo effect, whatever you want. But it works.

For some, that may be your high school, your dance school, or the field where you made that epic touchdown, any place that can help jog the memories you made there. The goal is to find somewhere you felt good and proud of yourself. And while you're there, remind yourself that you are still the person who achieved the greatness that you're reminiscing about there. Then, especially if there's a trophy or something symbolizing the success in the building, take time to go look at it.

In other cases, this might even be a certain person's gravesite. Sit down and have a chat with them. Tell them about who you are now, and maybe even leave a flower. You will feel good about paying your respects to a loved one.

For someone else, it might be the church you grew up in. If that's you, you likely felt comfort and safety while being there, so go again and reap the same benefits you did as a child.

Basically, anywhere that you feel called to should be where you go when in need of a deep breath, a reset, or a reminder of the past.

Loving yourself means taking time to do the things that you need to do to feel right, happy, and whole again.

Other places that may be significant to you are:

- The house where you grew up.

- The church or location where you got married.

- Your favorite park.

- A city or country you love going to.

- A coffee shop or restaurant that you frequent.

- The backyard of the babysitter's house you used to play in as a kid.

- A store you used to go into a lot with a parent growing up.

- The community center where you went to attend church events.

- Your family's favorite restaurant.

Stick with Your Roots—Celebrate Holidays with Your Family

Whether it's your family by blood or by choice, take the time to spend with them, especially around the holidays. As we've said in this book before, you never know how long you have someone around on earth for, so don't waste a single opportunity to be in their presence, to hear their laugh, and to just simply hug them.

If you can't afford to go home or logistically can't make it there for whatever reason, at least schedule a video call with them. It will make the hearts on both sides of the screen happy.

In a similar notion, if you have the means and space, please consider having people who do not have anywhere else to go on these big days come to your house. Many families have an "open door" policy for anyone who needs a place to go—and if yours isn't already like that, maybe that can be a nice new tradition that you do every year.

Looking back, you'll never regret the time you spent loving on others—you only risk regret if you don't have enough of it.

Discuss Your Life with Family and Friends

When it comes to the people you trust in your group of friends or in your family, you should feel free to discuss whatever is going on in your life with them. For one thing, if they care for and love you, they will want to know—especially in regard to your overall wellness. But it's also healthy to vent or get something outside of your body.

You've likely heard someone say it "felt good to get something off of their shoulders," and simply talking about a situation or problem often makes people feel like there's a weight lifted from themselves.

Moreover, talking with your loved ones about the good and the bad in your life helps you feel a sense of belonging and will improve your mental health. On the other hand, isolation and fighting battles on your own will not provide you with either of those benefits.

If you feel like you have a hard time opening up to your friends or family, here are some tips for getting closer to people:

- **Don't ever force things.** You must first develop a strong connection with someone before both parties are typically comfortable in engaging with one another about their personal lives. And a great way to get this ball rolling is by participating in an activity with a new friend—like tennis, swimming, going to a movie, or anything you both like to do—that does not afford much time for the pressure of conversation to kick in.

- **Bond over a new hobby.** Aside from the activities mentioned above, you can also go out of your comfort zone and start a new hobby in order to get to know someone better. You'll likely grow close over the initial struggle in the activity, but then you'll also celebrate each other's successes.

Don't Be Afraid to Ask for Help

This goes hand-in-hand with the above tip, but talking about your life and actually asking for help are two separate things.

The first can just be an information dump, and the second can actually trigger the person you're speaking with that you are asking for their assistance.

Aside from friends and family members, you can also go to these people to chat about your life and get additional resources:

- **Your School Advisers**
  If you're still in school, you probably have a special adviser assigned to you to help navigate the courses you should take. However, this person is also tuned into the community in and around campus, so they may be able to point you in the right direction regarding an issue you need help with.

- **Your Therapist**
  As we've already covered in this book, a therapist is a great third-party point of reference, who you can always (and should) bring your issues to for analysis.

- **Support Groups**
  Depending on what you're battling (the loss of someone close to you, mental health issues, substance use disorder, domestic abuse), there may be a local support group for people who are dealing with similar things that you can join.

- **Hotlines**
  Similar to the last point, there are also a ton of hotlines that you can call if you feel like you cannot or should not confide in someone already in your life. Your city's website may have a comprehensive list of these for you. Or you can text or call 988, and you'll be able to speak with a trained crisis counselor any time of day or night.

- **Online Chat Groups**
  This is also like the previous two points, but you should be especially careful with these and take extreme caution when meeting up with someone who you meet through a forum like that.

- **The Human Resources (HR) Department**
  If your issue has to do with the workplace, you should always go to HR. It is their job to make sure that employees are given the most supportive working environment possible.

- **Your Healthcare Provider**
  Your doctor is a wonderful person to go to if you are having issues in your life because they are experienced professionals and someone who (if you're over eighteen) legally cannot share your business with other people.

- **Religious or Spiritual Leaders**
  If you are someone who goes to church or are a part of some kind of spiritual group, reaching out to the leaders in these areas are also great people to turn to.

We hope this serves as a non-exhaustive list of people in your community and from around the entire world (if you're using hotlines or chat groups) who are available to help you. However, please also be advised that sometimes, the people you first go to for help are not emotionally or physically available. So, don't give up and keep trying until you find the right one.

And here are the steps for actually asking someone for help:

1. **Think about what you want.** What is it that you need? Help getting out of an abusive relationship? A referral for a chiropractor to address the knot you've had in your back

forever? Or do you just feel like dishing about your latest date? Whoever you're speaking to needs this context before you go any further.

2. **Decide who to talk to.** Depending on the issue you're looking to solve, it is appropriate for you to go to some people and not others. Say you're having a sexual obstacle with your partner—your mother is likely not the right person to go for that (*unless* you have an established relationship where sex is not off the table when it comes to sharing information together, but only you will know what each party is comfortable with). In the case that you would prefer not to share this with your mother, a friend, therapist, or doctor may be a better choice to address that problem. (Please refer to the list above.)

3. **Choose the right time and place.** So, you've singled out the result you want, you've decided who the right person will be to talk about it with, and now you need to find the right time and place to talk to that person about that particular topic. For instance, suppose you have an intimate question that you want to address with your therapist over the phone. Well, while you're in the middle of your office or around your family may not be the best time or place for that conversation. Instead, you might feel more open and honest while sitting alone in your room. The same thing goes for the other person as well. If they are not in a space to receive and respond to whatever you're asking for help with, their advice may not be authentic. Let's use the therapist example. You could first contact them by saying something like, "I'd like to schedule a time with you to discuss something personal and important. When would you have availability for that?" With that, both parties will know how to prepare for what is

to be discussed.

4. **Decide how to talk about it.** When you narrow down the issue, find the right person, and schedule the time in a setting you're both comfortable in, you'll next need to make sure that you are communicating effectively. This will require that you are calm, so taking several breaths may be necessary before you start talking. Then, you'll want to make sure to describe your feelings, thoughts, moods, and how your body feels. Basically, you want to give the other person a clear picture of your situation and what they would feel like if they were in it. And when it comes to answering any of their follow-up questions, you'll want to be as open and honest as you can be.

5. **Congratulate yourself.** Once you've completed all of these steps, take the time to celebrate that you just dedicated a lot of time and effort to your own well-being, and that is something that should be commended! Not everyone goes the extra mile in an attempt to better themselves or a situation they may be in, and if you did—that's a true way of showing love to yourself!

6. **Follow up and pay it forward.** Always thank the person for their support, provide follow-ups in terms of ways they can further help, or inquire if there are ways in which you can similarly help them in the future.

And please don't be afraid to try and try again. If you didn't get the reaction or advice you were looking for or what you got isn't sitting well with you, keep talking. This is especially important if you're looking for help with a substance use disorder, a health concern, or anything else that may require you to advocate for yourself until you get what you need.

However, if you're trying to find a support group, therapist, or doctor, and you haven't gotten anywhere using the methods above, there are also plenty of ways you can help yourself by using your laptop, borrowing a friend's computer, or going to the library. Do a simple search for the Substance Abuse and Mental Health Services Administration (SAMHSA.gov) to find support for your mental health, substance use disorder, and general wellness.

Seek Emotional Closeness with Family

Being emotionally close with a family member requires more than just feeling like you're on good terms or even friendly with someone. On the contrary, it requires a deep understanding of someone's struggles, what they celebrate in their lives, and how they feel about the things that have happened to them.

But this is not a one-way street. Emotional closeness will require that you too are open to sharing those things with a particular family member. If you're not sure if you're emotionally close to someone? Answer the following questions:

- Do you feel safe sharing your private issues and concerns with them?

- Do they make you feel supported and like they have your back?

- Do you feel like they can listen to you without judgment?

- Do you feel free and comfortable talking *to* them about something that is bothering you about them?

- Do you feel like they really want to hear about both the good and the bad things in your life?

- Do you care deeply about them and know they feel the same about you?

- Is it easy for you to shift from light to heavier conversations with them?

- Do you feel empathy toward them?

- Are you genuinely interested in what they have to say about their experiences, feelings, and relationships?

- Are you able to be fully present around them? (Without exterior distractions like your phone or other people).

- When they are hurting, do you feel compassion for them?

If you answered yes to all of these, you likely share an emotional closeness with whoever you were thinking about.

On the other hand, here are signs that you are not emotionally close to someone:

- You are afraid to share your most vulnerable feelings or embarrassing experiences.

- The relationship feels superficial.

- Even when you try to share, you don't feel seen, heard, or understood.

- You're often unsure where you stand with them, and you're often afraid of being criticized or judged by them.

- They often make you feel disappointed or let down.

- Your conversations with them are one-sided and focus mostly on them and their issues.

- It doesn't take long for the two of you to run out of things to talk about.

- You feel lonely in the relationship.

If you find yourself having an emotionally distant relationship with a family member and you want to take things deeper, try to talk to them about that. But if things are fine just the way they are, that's okay too. You can't be available and open to everyone—you'll lose steam really quickly. So, be picky and careful with the people who you are emotionally close with.

Check in on Your Growth Journals Often

The only way you'll be able to monitor your growth is through intentional reflection and reviewing your journals. You should revisit these as often as you need to.

And if you're having a particularly difficult day, go back and look at all of the progress you've made so far, and take the opportunity to feel proud of yourself. Even if it's a minor change, such as a goal to wear sunscreen every day, and you upheld that for an entire week, that's progress!.

Going back to your journals may also be a helpful way for you to forgive some of the things you wrote or wrote about doing in them.

Further, if you're the kind of person who likes to get every emotion and feeling out of your body about someone or something that you don't want to confront head-on, write a letter in your journal to the responsible parties without the intention of them ever reading it. This is a great way to get your feelings out of your body, and then you can move on. Then, these letters will serve as a reminder to you of the work you've done to forgive others as well.

Regardless of what you write in your growth journal, when you talk about yourself, your hopes, and your dreams, try to refrain from judgment. This is your space to be as open, raw, and vulnerable as possible, so take advantage of that and let the "word vomit" flow.

Moreover, try your best to use empowering words—even if you think the entry is about something negative. For example, suppose you're writing about how you allowed negative thoughts to take over your brain that day. Instead of focusing on the old habit sneaking back into your life, circle back to how you noticed the thoughts and redirected them to something more positive. Remember to talk to yourself like your own best friend…you would only encourage similar growth on behalf of your friends, right?

And don't forget gratitude, gratitude, gratitude! The more you practice being grateful for the things that are already in your lives, the better. Gratitude will attract even more positive things to happen all around you, while being stuck in the negative and playing the victim will do the exact opposite.

Also, don't be afraid to make your journal your own! If you're crafty, you can cut out magazine snippets, draw, or do anything else that you want to do inside of it. Again, it's your personal space. Make it something that you are attracted to and feel at home with.

Hold Yourself Accountable for Maintaining Your Goals

Just like the boundaries you set for others, you must also hold tight to the goals you set, and that means being accountable for making decisions that will help you achieve them.

For example, say you want to buy a house by the time you are thirty-five. It is your sole responsibility to make smart financial decisions in order to afford a down payment. So, depending on how much money you make and the goal budget you envision, you may need to make sure that in order to save up, you are going to have to avoid being frivolous—things like getting takeout or buying new clothes that you don't need—may need to be avoided. That also means that you may have to decline a fun night out with your friends.

It isn't always easy to deny yourself certain things, but that's the kind of commitment that is often required when a goal is to be met—especially a financial one.

A great way for you to hold yourself accountable is by creating a vision board to hang on your office wall or writing your goals right on your weekly calendar. Then, when someone asks you to do something or go somewhere, look at that board of words and ask, "Does that align with these goals?" If yes, go for it. If no, politely decline and move on with the rest of your day.

Chapter Eight

Final Thoughts

We hope you've been inspired to get out there and start loving the heck out of yourself! Remember that the goal is to be your best advocate and your own best friend, and that means that you are kind, understanding, and patient with yourself.

Reflection on the Journey of Navigating the Love You Have for Yourself, No Matter Your Personality

Regardless of whether you're a social butterfly, tend to keep to yourself, or enjoy a mixture of being out and at home, it's important for you to love yourself for the person that you are.

And the first step to doing that is changing your inner monologue to one that is not constantly criticizing and berating you—like so many of you have gotten into the habit of doing. Instead, lift yourself up, tell yourself that you're beautiful, and be proud of yourself for the small and big successes of the day.

In addition to the tips you've already read, another way you can get your self-love journey started is by writing "I love you" on a sticky note and attaching it to your bathroom mirror. Then, every morning and every night after you brush your teeth, focus in on your face so that you can only see your eyes and repeat to yourself, "I love you" ten times. The note should serve as a reminder for you to do this daily.

A similar exercise, if you don't like the sound of the previous one, requires you to brush your teeth with your nondominant hand and repeat, "I love you" ten times to yourself. The purpose for using the opposite hand is because, through that small change, you're activating your subconscious mind, and once you engrain the love you have for yourself in there, it will be almost impossible to go back on that.

You might feel foolish doing either of these at first, but the result is so worth it. We promise! Think about the person you love the most in this entire world...now imagine having those same heart-fluttering feelings about yourself! It's one of the greatest gifts you can give to yourself.

The Importance of Continuous Effort and Growth in Yourself

Please remember that this is a life-long journey, and if you find yourself going back to old patterns of hateful thoughts and feelings toward yourself, take a breath, forgive yourself, and then purposefully move your intentions to love.

And the person that you are will continually change as you grow and learn different lessons, so you may find that you have to love someone who is very different in a few years...and that's a good thing. If you didn't, you wouldn't be evolving, and a compassionate and curious person simply cannot resist evolution.

Also, please don't ever give up. This work can be hard, but that just goes to show you that it's worth it.

Embracing the Dynamic Nature of Love and the Beauty of Learning through the Differences We All Have

What's even more beautiful about learning to love yourself is that you can often do it through the experience of noting differences between yourself and other people—and simultaneously loving what you can bring to each other and to the world as a whole.

That's kind of a mouthful, so let's consider an example. Suppose you have a friend who is more on the reserved and insecure side, and you are outgoing and confident. Well, you can note these differences and feel proud of yourself for being someone who can hop in and advocate on behalf of that friend, when necessary, but also love your friend for being able to help you during the quiet moments. Life is all about balance, and you need everyone on this planet...otherwise they wouldn't be here. Now, whether you think god, the universe, or something else, put you and them on this earth, that's your business. But the fact that you all have a purpose is likely something you can agree with.

It's also important to note that love is a powerful feeling, and if you feel overwhelmed by the amount of love you feel for yourself, it's okay, but try to turn that fear into celebration. Love is dynamic, and love is a force that not much else can reckon with.

Encouragement to Evolve, Adapt, and Cherish Yourself—Always

So, it is our hope that you will walk away after reading this book and start seeing the world through a whole new lens—one that looks for all of the good in yourself and in your life.

But if you find that you could use another read-through, by all means, please do that. Or go back and mark sections that you found particularly impactful or meaningful.

Remember, this is a marathon, not a sprint. So, it's fine if the journey to loving yourself takes a bit and is constantly evolving and adapting to exactly where you are in life. And try not to give in to the feelings of doubt or envy of others. Because once you do, that is the energy that you will give off to others. (But please do not discount envy altogether. Instead of focusing on what others have that you do not, think of the feeling of envy as a way for you to know the goals that you want to achieve.)

At the end of the day, you are worth living the life of your dreams, and once you start consciously loving yourself, only good will follow!

So, if you see someone post on social media about buying a house, having a baby, or getting a new job, and you *feel* envious, thank god or the universe or whoever/whatever you believe in for showing you what you truly want in this life. Like with many of the things in this book, this isn't always easy—but it's something that gets easier with practice.

This more positive energy will create a positive frequency emanating from your being, and both will attract happiness into your life.

Appendices

Self-Assessment Questionnaire: Determine If You're a CD, MY, or Straddler

In the quest for self-understanding, recognizing one's intrinsic personality traits plays a crucial role. This self-assessment questionnaire has been carefully designed to help you discern whether you align most closely with the introspective nature of a Cave Dweller (CD), the extroverted inclinations of a Mountain Yeller (MY), or the balanced characteristics of a Straddler. By reflecting on your behaviors, preferences, and reactions in various situations, this tool aims to provide insight into your predominant personality type. Approach each question with honesty and openness, and remember, there's no right or wrong answer—just a deeper understanding of your unique self waiting to be unveiled.

Personality Indicator #1

Circle one answer per question.

50 WAYS TO LOVE YOURSELF

1. Have you ever walked in your sleep during your adult life?

   YES or NO

2. As a teenager, did you feel comfortable expressing your feelings to one or both of your parents?

   YES or NO

3. Do you have a tendency to look directly into a person's eyes when talking to them?

   YES or NO

4. Do you feel that most people, when you first meet them, are uncritical of your appearance?

   YES or NO

5. In a group situation with people you've just met, would you feel comfortable drawing attention to yourself by initiating a conversation?

   YES or NO

6. Do you feel comfortable holding hands or hugging someone you're in a relationship with in front of other people?

   YES or NO

7. When someone talks about feeling warm physically, do you begin to feel warm also?

   YES or NO

8. Do you tend to tune out when someone is talking to you because you're anxious to come up with your side of the story?

YES or NO

9. Do you feel that you learn better by seeing and/or reading than by hearing?

YES or NO

10. In a new class or company meeting, do you usually feel comfortable asking questions in front of the group?

YES or NO

11. When expressing your ideas, do you find it important to relate all the details leading up to the subject so the other person can understand it completely?

YES or NO

12. Do you enjoy relating to children?

YES or NO

13. Are you comfortable with your body movements when faced with unfamiliar people and circumstances?

YES or NO

14. Do you prefer reading fiction rather than non-fiction?

YES or NO

50 WAYS TO LOVE YOURSELF

15. If you were to imagine sucking on a juicy lemon, would your mouth water?

    YES or NO

16. Do you feel comfortable receiving a compliment in front of other people?

    YES or NO

17. Do you feel that you're a good conversationalist?

    YES or NO

18. Do you feel comfortable when complimentary attention is drawn to your physical body?

    YES or NO

Personality Indicator #2

Circle one answer per question.

1. Have you ever awakened in the middle of the night and felt that you could not move your body and/or talk?

   YES or NO

2. As a child, did you feel you were more affected by your parents' tone of voice than by what they actually said?

   YES or NO

3. If someone you know talks about a fear that you've

experienced before, do you have a tendency to re-experience that apprehension or fear?

YES or NO

4. After having an argument with someone, do you tend to dwell on what you could or should have said?

YES or NO

5. Do you tend to occasionally tune out when someone is talking to you and, therefore, don't hear what's being said because your mind drifts to something totally unrelated?

YES or NO

6. Do you sometimes desire to be complimented for a job well done but feel embarrassed or uncomfortable when complemented?

YES or NO

7. Do you often fear not being able to carry on a conversation with someone you've just met?

YES or NO

8. Do you feel self-conscious when attention is drawn to your physical body or appearance?

YES or NO

9. If you had a choice, would you rather avoid being around children most of the time?

YES or NO

10. Do you feel uptight in body movements, especially when faced with unfamiliar people or circumstances?

YES or NO

11. Do you prefer reading non-fiction rather than fiction?

YES or NO

12. If someone describes a very bitter taste, do you have difficulty experiencing the physical feeling of that bitter taste?

YES or NO

13. Do you generally feel that you see yourself less favorably than others see you?

YES or NO

14. Do you tend to feel awkward or self-conscious holding hands and/or kissing someone you're in a relationship with in front of other people?

YES or NO

15. In a new lecture or company meeting, do you usually feel uncomfortable asking questions in front of the group?

YES or NO

16. Do you feel uneasy if someone you've just met looks you

directly in the eyes when talking to you, especially if the conversation is about you?

YES or NO

17. In a group situation with people you've just met, would you feel uncomfortable drawing attention to yourself by initiating a conversation?

YES or NO

18. If you're in a relationship or are very close to someone, do you find it difficult or embarrassing to verbalize your love for them?

YES or NO

Personality Indicator Scores

Personality Indicator #1

- Give yourself 10 points for every YES answer for questions one and two.

- Give yourself 5 points for every YES answer for questions three through eighteen.

- Write the total number at the top of #1's questionnaire.

Personality Indicator #2

- Give yourself 10 points for every YES answer for questions one and two.

- Give yourself 5 points for every YES answer for questions three through eighteen.

- Write the total number at the top of #2's questionnaire.

- Combine the total from Personality Indicators #1 and #2.

Using the Scoring Chart

On the scoring chart, look up the combined score of Personality Indicators #1 and #2 on the HORIZONTAL axis of the chart and circle the number.

- Take the total score of Personality Indicator #1, locate it on the VERTICAL axis of the chart, and circle the number.

- Draw a horizontal line across the page from the Personality Indicator #1 score, then draw a vertical line down from the combined score.

- The number in the box where the two lines intersect represents your true, adjusted percentage personality indicator.

- Scores 61 and higher indicate a Mountain Yeller personality type.

- Scores 45 and lower indicate a Cave Dweller personality type.

- Scores 47 to 56 indicate a Straddler personality type.

Cave Dweller Tendencies

- Reserved
- Head ruled
- Controlling
- Wants space and security
- Prefers socializing one-on-one
- Singular focus
- Thinks before reacting
- Prefers showing affection privately
- Distrusts flattery
- Enjoys working alone
- Enjoys individual activities
- Wants alone time
- Dresses for comfort
- Decides after thinking about it
- Speaks literally, to the point
- Infers from what others say
- Feels emotional pain in the mind

- Fears loss of security

Cave Dweller Priorities

- Career/Financial Security
- Hobbies/Children
- Relationships/Family
- Sex/Lovers

Mountain Yeller Tendencies

- Outgoing
- Heart ruled
- Dominating
- Wants connection and touch
- Enjoys socializing in groups
- Movement focused
- Reacts spontaneously
- Comfortable with affection anytime
- Likes reassurance and compliments
- Enjoys working with people
- Enjoys team activities

- Wants to be together as much as possible
- Decides in the moment
- Speaks inferentially—adds story
- Takes literally what others say
- Feels emotional pain in body and mind
- Fears rejection

Mountain Yeller Priorities

- Relationships/Sex
- Family/Children
- Friends/Hobbies
- Career/Financial security

COMBINED SCORE #1 AND #2

SCORE #1	50	55	60	65	70	75	80	85	90	95	100	105	110	115	120	125	130	135	140	145	150	155	160	165	170	175	180	185	190	195	200
100											100	95	91	87	83	80	77	74	71	69	67	65	63	61	59	57	56	54	53	51	50
95										100	95	90	86	83	79	76	73	70	68	66	63	61	59	58	56	54	53	51	50	49	48
90									100	95	90	86	82	78	75	72	69	67	64	62	60	58	56	55	53	51	50	49	47	46	45
85								100	94	89	85	81	77	74	71	68	65	63	61	59	57	55	53	52	50	49	47	46	45	44	43
80							100	94	89	84	80	76	73	70	67	64	62	59	57	55	53	52	50	48	47	46	44	43	42	41	40
75						100	94	88	83	79	75	71	68	65	63	60	58	56	54	52	50	48	47	45	44	43	42	41	39	38	38
70					100	93	88	82	78	74	70	67	64	61	58	56	54	52	50	48	47	45	44	42	41	40	39	38	37	36	35
65				100	93	87	81	76	72	68	65	62	59	57	54	52	50	48	46	45	43	42	41	39	38	37	36	35	34	33	33
60			100	92	86	80	75	71	67	63	60	57	55	52	50	48	46	44	43	41	40	39	38	36	35	34	33	32	32	31	30
55		100	92	85	79	73	69	65	61	58	55	52	50	48	46	44	42	41	39	38	37	35	34	33	32	31	31	30	29	28	28
50	100	91	83	77	71	67	62	59	56	53	50	48	45	43	42	40	38	37	36	34	33	32	31	30	29	29	28	27	26	26	25
45	90	82	75	69	64	60	56	53	50	47	45	43	41	39	38	36	35	33	32	31	30	29	28	27	26	26	25	24	24	23	23
40	80	73	67	62	57	53	50	47	44	42	40	38	36	35	33	32	31	30	29	28	27	26	25	24	24	23	22	22	21	21	20
35	70	64	58	54	50	47	44	41	39	37	35	33	32	30	29	28	27	26	25	24	23	23	22	21	20	19	19	18	18	18
30	60	55	50	46	43	40	38	35	33	32	30	29	27	26	25	24	23	22	21	20	19	19	18	18	17	17	16	16	15	15
25	50	45	42	38	36	33	31	29	28	26	25	24	23	22	21	20	19	19	18	17	16	16	15	15	14	14	14	13	13	13
20	40	36	33	31	29	27	25	24	22	21	20	19	18	17	17	16	15	15	14	14	13	13	13	12	12	11	11	11	11	10	10
15	30	27	25	23	21	20	19	18	17	16	15	14	14	13	13	12	11	11	10	10	10	9	9	9	9	9	8	8
10	20	18	17	15	14	13	13	12	11	11	10	10	9	9	8	8	7	7	7	7	5	6	6	6	6	6	5	5
5	10	9	8	8	7	7	6	6	6	5	5	5	5	4	4	4	4	4	3	3	3	3	3	3	3	3	3	3	3	3	5
0	0	0	0	0	0	0	0	0	0	0	0	0	0	0	0	0	0	0	0	0	0	0	0	0	0	0	0	0	0	0	0

About the Author

Dr. Cline lives with her husband, two daughters, two German Shepherds, and two Yorkies in the hills of North Carolina. Her expertise in relationship building has offered her the opportunity to travel around the world as a keynote speaker and international workshop facilitator.

www.ingramcontent.com/pod-product-compliance
Lightning Source LLC
Chambersburg PA
CBHW070109080526
44586CB00013B/1243